# Discovering The Borders 2

## Other titles in this series

# Discovering
# The Borders 2

ALAN SPENCE

JOHN DONALD PUBLISHERS LTD
EDINBURGH

ISBN 0 85976 377 3

*British Library Cataloguing in Publication Data*
A catalogue record for this book is available from
the British Library.

Typeset by ROM-Data Corporation Ltd., Falmouth, Cornwall.
Printed & bound in Great Britain by Bell & Bain Ltd., Glasgow.

# Acknowledgements

Once again my thanks to all who have assisted me in compiling this book; it is impossible to give each individual mention. The following authors have allowed me to quote from their published work, so a special thanks to Walter Elliot and John Randall. Also to the Hon. Patrica Maxwell Scott for permission to use quotations from Sir Walter and to Viv Billingham, formerly of Tweedhope Sheepdogs, and author of three books on the Border Collie.

# Introduction

Once again it has given me the greatest of pleasure to collect the information for this, the second book on the Borders. Complete strangers have answered my telephone queries, allowed me to quote from their own work, and allowed me access to their private property.

The text encourages readers to depart from the main roads in some instances, but I would ask you to take the utmost care when driving over unfenced hill roads; the sheep and stock which may be encountered are the lifeblood of the border farmers. 'Beware of the lambs' notices are there for the benefit of sheep, not motorists.

Walkers should acquaint themselves with the 'Country Code', especially where dogs are concerned; take from the Border Hills nothing but a photograph, and leave only your footprint.

# Contents

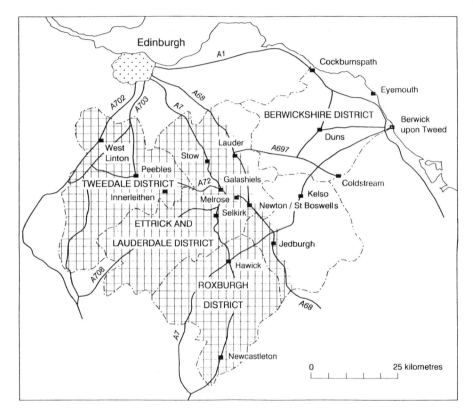

Location Map

# CHAPTER 1

## *The Place*

Whaur sall I enter the Promised Land,
Ower Sutra or doun the Lyne,
Up the side o' the water o' Clyde,
Or cross the muirs at the heid o' Tyne,
Or staucherin' on by Crawfordjohn,
Yont the Glens whaur Tweed rins wee? —
Its a maitter sma' whaur your road may fa'
Gin it land ye safe in the South Countrie.

Those words of John Buchan, the first Lord Tweedsmuir, give a clue to the appearance of this part of the Borders. By all his chosen routes into Tweeddale — the Promised Land — his footsteps were never going to be far from heather-covered moorland or a winding hill burn.

This book seeks to 'discover' the Border country beyond but including the upper valley of the Tweed. This, to many people is the the Border heartland, the hills and moorlands forming part of the Southern Uplands, comprising the Lammermuirs, Cheviot, Moorfoots and Tweedsmuir Ranges. Those hills were formed mainly when earth movements forced ancient sedimentary rocks upwards into mighty mountain ranges. Natural forces ground these down, before further earth movements again raised them, wind and weather plus an ice age or two have finally left us with the familiar rounded hills so typical of southern Scotland.

Volcanic rocks can be found protruding through the sedimentary layers at several places, one of the most obvious being Rubers Law, near Hawick, where this ancient volcano's basaltic heart penetrates the Old Red Sandstone. The Scottish - English Border west of the Carter Bar as dealt with in this book follows the watershed of the Cheviots. Here in the western section of this range the hidden granite heart of the eastern is replaced with sandstone which frequently protrudes in small craggy outcrops. Here on bleak Carter Fell is one of the few places where coal was exploited in the Borders, beside the now filled

The rounded Border Hills viewed from a point between Ettrick and Yarrow

in shafts or pits can still be found fragments of soft brown coal but there is little sign that this has been anything other than a small time operation. Whatever their composition the hills of the Border country all share the same smooth rounded shape so typical of southern Scotland, with only the occasional glimpse of crag or scree.

Parts of this book reach areas not usually associated with the Borders, but the criterion is the boundary of the Borders Regional Council. Like the remainder of Scotland the Borders area was, as the buzz word was at the time, 'regionalised' in 1975. Swept asunder were the county and burgh councils, the latter much lamented as their existence carried a fair share of local civic pride. Borderers were fond of their toon cooncils, the provost, burgh treasurer and officials — the toon clerk and burgh surveyor always at hand to buttonhole with a complaint. Despite having representatives at both region and district level, and local offices for both in most of the former burghs, the seat of power now seems that little bit more remote.

District Councils replaced the county councils. There was some juggling with boundaries while the shires of Peebles and Selkirk were replaced with Tweeddale and Ettrick and Lauderdale districts. This book covers these two and part of Roxburgh district, the fourth district within the Borders Region,

Berwickshire having been dealt with in its entirety in *Discovering the Borders 1*.

When, in 1993, Ian Lang, the Secretary of State for Scotland, announced his new proposals for local government, it appeared as if the Borders in their previous form would be destroyed. Lang was to learn a lesson taught to politicians, rulers, and administrators down through the centuries that attempts to meddle with and destroy the Borders can only have one result — dismal failure. Traditionally this was the old Eastern and Middle Marches, later to be known as Berwickshire, Roxburghshire, Selkirkshire, and Peebleshire. Lang, somewhat misinformed by his grass-roots supporters, proposed to remove Berwickshire from the Borders and incorporate it with East Lothian into a newly invented local authority. This awoke a sleeping giant in The Borders, where the electorate right across the political spectrum protested long and loud against any interference in the *status quo* of the Borders Region.

The term 'Borders' is a fairly recent one, its use usually indicating the country north of the Anglo-Scottish border proper. One of the earliest uses of 'Borders' is found in a book by the Rev. Richard Warren published in 1802, *A Tour through the Northern Counties of England and the Borders of Scotland.* Around the same time Scott was working on his *Minstrelsy of the Scottish Borders*, bringing the term into popular usage.

Therefore the cattle reivers, the shepherds, the millers, smiths, weavers and tanners down through history were not Borderers by this name; they were, if any collective term is to be applied to the residents of the counties of the boundary with England, 'March men'.

In medieval times this Scottish 'Middle March' stretched from Kershopefoot in Liddesdale east along the Cheviot's backbone to the boundary with the Merse or the Eastern March, which was approximately the old county of Berwickshire. *Discovering the Borders 2* starts at Soutra Hill to foray towards Penicuik and Edinburgh at Leadburn, touching at one point the Pentlands. Zigzagging north-west the regional boundary finally swings southwards towards Moffat from the Bore Stane. Above Moffatdale the line deviates eastwards above the crags of White Coombe and Lochcraig Head overlooking Loch Skeen.

This is a mere feint, as soon, following the watersheds, this boundary continues its wending way south-west between Borders Region and Dumfries and Galloway until it picks up the Border proper, near Kershopefoot on the Liddel Water. Now the region line is also that of the Border marching, south-west through Kershope Forest, part of the Borders Forest Park, to Larriston Fells, Kielder, Wauchope and the Carter Bar where *Discovering the Borders 1* takes over.

Sometimes the Borders is known as the 'Scott country', because of the association with Sir Walter with the area where he lived, worked, travelled and wrote, his pen touching many a remote valley and riverside burgh. Although his novels and poetical works covered areas far outwith the Border hills, his associations around the Tweed and its tributaries are stronger here than anywhere else. Whenever the name Scott appears on its own in the following pages the reference is to Sir Walter. During his lifetime Scott collected many old tales and ballads from existing manuscripts and the dying oral tradition, losing in the writing some of their character if his friend, the Ettrick Shepherd's mother, is to be believed, but preserving them for future generations to enjoy and ponder upon.

It must be said that Scott was prejudiced in favour of his own family name, and the Dukes of Buccleuch. Where Scott had several versions of a traditional ballad to choose from for publication, his choice was always the one which showed the family in the best light. Today some authorities suspect Scott of having been the author of some of his 'traditional' ballads. Contemporary reports, (see *Discovering the Borders 1*) on Scott's funeral, give it as a day of national and local mourning. Yet it appears that sometimes his ambitions led to some mockery by the populace. When he attempted to buy Darnick Tower near Melrose he was sometimes referred to as the 'Duke of Darnick', while from distant glens scribes wrote, 'traditional' ballads and sent them to Scott as the genuine article.

Nevertheless the man's contribution to recording the culture of the people of the Border valleys was enormous. Add these to Scott's own prolific writings, which created a land of tower and castle, prancing war horse, noble knight and winsome lady laying the foundations for a tourist industry which began in his own time and continues to this day.

Border Ballads can be divided into two categories, as Scott

did in his *Minstrelsy*. These are the Historic Ballad and the Romantic Ballad, the former usually dealing with some deed of derring do — a raid across the Border — the rescue from an English prison of a fellow Borderer. Death and murder are found in the Historic Ballad, but the real gory stuff is in the Romantic Ballad. In most the hero dies, sometimes along with the heroine, after hacking down innumerable members of her family. Sons slay their father after discovering that he had been the murderer of the mother — all the very stuff of romance. Scott's *Minstrelsy* includes a further chapter, 'Imitations of the Ancient Ballad', including work by himself, John Leyden and other contemporaries.

This is not a densely populated part of Scotland. The Borders Region, with 103,000 inhabitants, forms a mere two per cent of the Scottish total. Even this is deceptive, as the majority of these dwell in a handful of major centres where the thread of Tweed or its tributaries bisect the Border hills.

Among the hills and valleys there is a marked difference in land use from further east in the bowl of the Merse, where the cereal rules supreme. Here in the upland areas the trend is more towards stock rearing and growing crops to support this enterprise, be that crop hay, silage or the rough grazing of grass and heather upon the hilltops. Many tombstones, in country churchyards bear the simple legend, 'Shepherd' as memorials to men who went to the hill in all weathers, their sole protection from wind and rain a plaid in shepherd's check. Special 'sprung' boots with turned up toes and curved sole carried the 'herds' as shepherds are invariably called in the Borders, over moss, and bent with deceptive ease.

There is nothing 'nine till five' about the job of the stock farmer or shepherd. Always the flock comes first; rain, hail or raging blizzard the charges must be tended seven days a week. There are busy times and busier times for the shepherd, for a full twal month. During winter the meagre grazing must be supplemented by hay and concentrated feeds. Come snow, the job is all the more difficult, but the task is made easier today with the, 'quads' or four-wheel motor bikes which for most hill shepherds have replaced the sprung boots of past generations. Yet there are still parts of the hill which no vehicle can reach, and conditions when only Shank's pony will reach outlying flocks awaiting their hay from the small barns at strategic sites.

Lambing time is the sheepfarmer's harvest, starting on the low ground with the Cheviots or one of their cross-breeds in March but extending into April for the hill places. Wet is the enemy of the newborn lamb; be it cold but dry, the ewe will find shelter somewhere for her newborn offspring. A succession of wet days, 'perish' the new arrivals unless the shepherd can get the lambs undercover, which on hill farms is far from easy.

As in any outdoor trade the weather is the ruling factor, such as the first two days of April, 1992, when two days of sleet and snow cut short all thoughts of spring. It caught the low ground lambing right at its peak; rivers rose to levels not reached for decades, while thousands of lambs perished in the fields. As if that were not enough, a plague of caterpillars devastated much of the grazing in the upper Ettrick valley in early summer, just when it was becoming vital for ewes recovering from the rigours of lambing.

Sheep which have spent their lives grazing upon hill pasturage could well be described as an organic product. Heather, grass and upland herbs form their diet on a terrain untouched by pesticides or insecticides; the hill sheep themselves are only subject to the minimum of medication. Although the wool clip is today of lesser importance to the hill farmers income, it remains the second most important event in the shepherding year, the fleeces from Border flocks yielding around 15 per cent of the annual Scottish wool crop. Then dipping to prevent an infestation of maggots spaening; i.e., separating the ewes and lambs, whereafter, for nights on end the separated flocks bleat for each other across the hill. Not to mention foot trimming or dosing for the many ills which can affect sheep — it's nae holiday bein' a herd.

A change has come to the Border hills in the late decades of the twentieth century, where for eons blackfaced sheep ruled supreme. These successors to the early 'forest sheep' have been ousted from many of their old haunts by man-made forestry. Conifers in one form or another have changed the ecology of thousands of upland acres. Where once among the bare bleak peat hags the curlew's call betrayed fugitive Covenanters, thickets of Norway Spruce would today conceal a regiment.

Planting these new forests has meant extensive drainage

Afforestation on the Border hills in the upper part of Slitrig, also shows the 'Catrail' running across the picture in 'firebreaks'.

programmes, allowing water to drain from the peat blanket which had the sponge-like ability to soak up prodigious rainfall. Water was released only gradually, thereby maintaining good flows of water in the Tweed system even in periods of low rainfall. Today river levels rise rapidly following heavy rainfall; equally dramatically they shrink again with the onset of dry weather.

Gone in the wake of the forestry in many instances is a way of life, commemorated by the ruined shepherds' cottages and sheep stells now deep in forestry plantations, where the chainsaw's buzz will one day replace the herd's whistle guiding his Border collie out and around the distant flocks. Stories are legendary about the intelligence of this remarkable breed of dog, which is only really at home on hill or pasture engaged in the job for which it was bred.

Without the assistance of the Border Collie the work of the shepherd would be well nigh impossible, especially in the far reaches of the upland country. A breed of working dog not only appreciated in Britain but worldwide wherever sheep are reared. Evolved from a number of breeds, all of which have contributed to characteristics which make the Border Collie what it is today. Colour would at first seem to be the least important, the most prevalent in the working breed coming in a combination of black and white. Either of these colours is usually visible at a distance regardless of the type of terrain, the

season or weather conditions. Pointers, setters and spaniels have
all made their contribution to the breed which was evolving in
the latter part of the nineteenth century when it was known as
the Scotch Colley. The key appears to have been one Adam
Telfer's dog, Old Hemp, which is considered to be the vital link
in the progression between the rough herding dogs and the
present day collie.

A Border Collie of true working stock is capable of running
a hundred miles a day, and indeed often does so the pent up
energy in such a strain makes it unsuitable for a pet, pathetically
taken for walks on the end of a lead. Even when well trained
the Border Collie is something of a free spirit, expected to work
on the hill on its own initiative at times out of sight and sound
of the handler. The trained shepherd's dog is not forever
looking over its shoulder for commands or hand signals; the
whistle is enough when within hearing, the blasts for the hill
dog being more rapid and urgent than those for the low ground
dog.

Afforestation is but another phase, an ongoing change in land
use and landscape, as the Rev. Andrew Handyside writing in the
*Statistical Account* under 'Miscellaneous Observations' notes:

> A great part of the land in Lyne and Megget has been formerly covered
> with wood, yet at present, there are only a few trees around the manse
> and farm houses. The old trees naturally decay through time, and the
> growth of young ones is effectually prevented by the sheep and cattle.

No modern plantation can have the visual appeal of the
natural woodland which once clothed the Border hills, the
scrub oaks, Scots pine, birch and rowan, the open type of
woodland which formed the Ettrick Forest, the haunt and
hunting ground of Scottish kings. Today, the farmer and the
shepherd mourn the loss of so many grazing hill acres, the hill
walker curses the barrier of sharp-needled Norway Spruce which
hinder his wanderings from valley to valley, while the professional forester rejoices in the tidy appearance of his modern
plantations.

Depopulation from the upland valleys is not a new phenom-
enon, again the Rev. Andrew Handyside of Lyne and Megget
Parishes describes the 'Cause of Depopulation' as follows: 'The

causes commonly assigned for the decrease in population in this district, are the demolition of cottages, and the junction of sheep farms'. The theme of sheep rearing replacing arable farming and even two hundred years ago the amalgamation of small farms into larger units. The latter a theme which continues to this day. While there were not the traumatic forced Clearances of the inhabitants of the Border valleys as was the case in the Highland glens, agricultural improvements and the trend to sheep farming reduced rural populations in outlying areas during the eighteenth century.

As always it is the industry of *homo sapiens* which has brought change upon the landscape. A change set in motion when the first tree fell before a stone axe, or when the first domesticated goat nibbled a sapling sprouting from the forest floor. Little remains to mark the passing of these early fishermen and hunters, their dwellings temporary, their artifacts few other than their stone tools and implements.

Repairing a drystone dyke at Henderland — another of man's influences on the Border landscape. Dykes in the valleys may contain the walls of some one time towers.

The diverse man-made and natural habitat found within this part of the Borders supports a wide range of flora and fauna. River and loch, moor and mire, heather and heath all have their part to play in the Region's ecology. Old and new woodland forms a haven for the roe deer whose numbers are on the increase; feral goats frequent the Cheviots and the moors above Moffat Dale. Otters are present along the riverbanks, although they are not as plentiful as the feral mink who have made the banks of the Tweed and its feeder streams very much their own. Foxes abound in wood and hill while badger populations are larger than most people suspect.

Here in the western upland area which provides a barrier to the prevailing wind, it is not surprising that rainfall is heavier than further east. Moist wet clouds swept across the Atlantic by the prevailing winds deposit their load upon the hills around upper Tweed, Teviot, Ettrick and Yarrow. It is well known that rain with winds from a westerly direction can fetch the Tweed down in flood, sometimes raging brown and dirty when scarce a drop of rain has fallen on the Merse.

It is not strictly true to say that all the rain falling in the Tweed catchment area reaches the sea at Berwick-upon-Tweed. Water

Abundant clean river water was an essential ingredient in the early Borders woolen industry.

reservoirs are another change in the landscape. The first was established at Tala. These now hold and supply water for the good citizens of Edinburgh to add to their dram, wash or cook with — in fact, some millions of gallons annually are diverted away from the Tweed system, where in the opinion of dedicated anglers, at least, it would be better employed by having fish swim around in it. Where catchment areas are concerned there are exceptions from that of the Tweed within the Borders Region, such as the river Liddel and its tributaries winding west by the Esk ultimately to discharge into the Atlantic through the Solway Firth.

An abundant water supply played its part in the establishment of the Borders woollen industry, both for washing fleeces and providing power for the early mills. Washing was certainly necessary before fleeces could be spun and woven, as it was the practice over many centuries for sheep to be coated with a primitive 'sheep dip' of a butter and tar mix as a protection from weather and disease.

It was only in a few instances that the water of the main river was harnessed when woollen manufacture was being transformed from a cottage to a factory industry. Rather it was from Tweed's tributaries that water power was derived; the Teviot and Slitrig at Hawick, the Ettrick at Selkirk and the mills ranked upstream of each other beside the Gala Water at Galashiels. The river Tweed did provide power upstream of Galashiels at Walkerburn and Peebles, but mainly in spinning and weaving the moving force came from tributaries.

Somewhere sometime a clerk mis-spelt the word 'twill', a description of a type of cloth produced in the Borders, as 'tweed' associating ever after the river and the cloth. Although founded on locally produced wool, this has figured less and less in the products of the Borders textiles and knitwear. Shared by the two industries however is a drop in demand for their products in the early part of the 1990s, brought about by economic factors far beyond the control of those who live in the mill towns and valley heads.

While the large-scale production of woven textiles aimed at a mass market has declined in the Border mill towns the trade is by no means dead. Spinning, weaving and knitting still continue in the towns beside Tweed, Teviot, Ettrick and the

Gala Water; today their products are mostly aimed at the upper end of the market.

From world-wide sources the finest of raw materials arrive at the Border mills to be sorted, spun and dyed ready to be woven or knitted into garments whose quality ensures a continued international reputation for 'Made in the Scottish Borders'. Mohair, alpaca, camel hair all find their way to the Borders, not forgetting the most luxurious of them all — cashmere.

Among the high mountains of Central Asia nomadic goat herds comb their charges when they are about to moult, the prize being a few ounces of underhair grown by the animals as a protective insulation against the bitter cold. After the journey half-way round the world, and many processes, the resulting cashmere garments will grace the backs of the famous and wealthy from London to New York and from San Francisco to Tokyo.

Visitors interested in following 'The Scottish Borders Woollen Trail' can do so with the aid of a free booklet with the above title available at Borders Tourist Offices. Included in, 'The Trail' are working mills, mill shops and museums which feature the history of Borders' textiles. For the full list of firms engaged in spinning, dyeing, weaving and knitting the Borders Regional Council produce a glossy brochure dealing with all the textile firms in the region. These range from hand-knitters with a limited output to the largest firms — themselves now part of international companies, where the potential weekly output is measured in thousands of garments.

The Borders were the playground of the Scottish kings, right down to the Stewarts, Ettrick Forest being for long a Royal Hunting Forest. 'To Peebles for the play' said King James: Without a doubt the Scottish Royals were fond of the Borders. Yet there was other quarry than the roe and deer for the hounds to pursue, or wildfowl and moorgame for the stooping hawk. Sometimes it was human prey the royal parties hunted, especially during the sixteenth century when the lawless activities of the Border clans required curbing.

These, the fabled Border Reivers, depending upon the personal viewpoint, could be cited as medieval muggers, local heroes, extortionists or patriots. It makes a romantic picture, coloured by romantic writers, of the mounted Scots or English bands crossing the Border by moonlight into enemy country to steal livestock. At grass-roots level there was little thought of national loyalty by the participants. First on the list when it came to dedication to duty was the close family, then the home valley, and some fellow Borderers followed far behind by any love for a Scottish ruler sitting in distant Edinburgh or Stirling while those in the Border valleys took the flak.

Yet even in other parts of the March country the inhabitants did not appreciate the goings-on of those right against the south-west corner of the Middle March, such as in *Maitland's Complaynt, Aganis the Thievis of Liddisdail*:

> Of Liddisdail the commoun theifis
> Sa peartlie steillis now and reifs,
> That nane may keep
> Horse, nolt, nor scheip,
> Norr yett dar sleip
> For their mischeifis.

> Thay theifis have neirhand herreit hail,
> Ettricke forest and Lawderdail;
> Now are they gane,
> In Lawthiane;
> And spairis nane
> That they will waill.

> He is weil kend, John of the Syde;
> A greater theif did never ryde.

John of the Side will be encountered later, in the chapter on Liddesdale, but Maitland's poem could hardly be described as an appreciation from one Scottish Borderer for the exploits of others.

For the people of Northumberland and Cumberland the situation was little better from a safe distance. Neither Henry VIII nor Good Queen Bess, as the ultimate English sovereign was known, need fear for their life or property in the full moon of a late autumn night. Well could their Borderers be left to get on with things, fending as best they could, creating an independent spirit, a spirit shared by their Scottish counter-

Kershopefoot in Liddesdale, one of the meeting places on 'days of truce'.

parts. Accounts of the immediate aftermath of the Battle of Flodden tell of the Borderers of Tyne and Teviotdale doing rather well from plundering the dead. According to the Bishop of Durham even the baggage of the victorious English army was not safe; the Bishop considered that the English Borderers did more harm to their own side than the Scots had done.

This then was frontier country, during the same century as Shakespeare was penning many a sonnet, and Europeans were bent upon wiping out the native peoples of the Americas. It was a different story on the Marches; here was the wild west without the Colt and Winchester, Beruit sans Klashniakov, which thankfully were not available. Deadly as the Borderers were with spear and sword, axe or close-quarter dirk their firearms were primitive — what joy they would have found in the modern weapons of destruction.

Yet both Stewarts and Tudors used their respective Border clans to their own advantage, at times encouraging their activities or enlisting the aid of their special qualities as light cavalry in times of war. At other times they punished, when rulers felt uneasy that some of the clan chiefs were aspiring to be kings themselves, or when periods of less warlike relationships prevailed between the two nations.

The Middle Marches in the 1500s brought some complex

14

relationships back and forth across the Border. Laws prohibiting cross-Border marriages seem to have been pretty well ignored, while night-time raiders might enjoy the hostelries of Carlisle by day, or attend horse races and football matches. Chroniclers record how conscripted Borderers from both sides wore emblems of recognition and merely fenced with each other. Apparently to kill a known 'enemy' could initiate a blood feud which could last for generations and was to be avoided at all costs.

To keep the peace when required, a system of wardenship was developed splitting the Anglo-Scottish Border into three sections, the East, Middle and West Marches. Scottish and English wardens were appointed for each march who were supposed to meet on 'days of truce' at specified places along the Border. The aim of these meetings was the settlement of grievances between the inhabitants of their respective marches north and south of the Border. Both factions were supposed to abide by a specific set of laws especially formatted for the keeping of peace and order between Scotland and England.

*Leges Marchiarum* — the March Laws, sought to provide redress for an injured party through the warden system. An Englishman who had been robbed would bring the complaint to the attention of his warden; he in turn would raise the matter with his Scottish counterpart who was duty bound to instigate further enquiries. If these enquiries were proven to be well founded the person responsible would be called upon to attend the next wardens' meeting on a day of truce to answer the charges.

Complicated procedures were also in operation for the recovery of stolen property where robbers could be pursued by 'hot trod' with a smouldering turf on spear point, or 'cold trod' which had to be instigated within six days, otherwise it would be adjudged to be a revenge raid, which, in the eyes of *Leges Marchiarum*, was an entirely different matter.

In addition to the three Scottish Wardens there was the appointment of 'The Keeper of Liddesdale' based at Hermitage Castle, in an attempt to control what was the most notorious valley of all. Wardenship must have been an unenviable task in the face of the Border freebooters who thought little of national patriotism when faced with the choice of what would yield the best profits. Cattle stealing, house burning, murder, or the theft of insight (household) goods did not require the perpetrator to cross between Scotland and England but could well be carried out against fellow countrymen.

Family feuds developed to complicate matters even between different family branches bearing the same surname; yet while their countries could be making warlike gestures, the people of Liddesdale and Redesdale might very well be on the best of terms plotting in what way they could exploit the situation.

When, in 1544, Hereford, on Henry VIII's instructions, devastated the Scottish Borderland in the 'rough wooing', burning cot and castle, he was aided in no small measure by Scots from the Middle Marches. Harried from all sides, the two centuries prior to their Union of the Crowns must have been a difficult time for the ordinary people of the Borders who wished only to get on with their lives without the interruption of fire and sword at regular intervals.

Blackmail was another invention of the great robber chiefs of the Borders, meaning black rent or, as would be seen today, protection money — a matter which the Scotts and Armstrongs could have given the Chicago gangsters some instruction upon. This practice receives mention in the ballad, *Jamie Telfer in the Fair Dodhead*. Jamie is seeking help after being robbed by the captain of Bewcastle.

> And when he came to the fair tower yett,
> He shouted loud, and cried weel hie,
> Till out bespak auld Gibby Elliot —
> 'Whae's this that brings the fray tae me.'

> 'It's I, Jamie Telfer o' the Fair Dodhead,
> And a harried man I think I be!
> There's naething left at the fair Dodhead,
> But a waefu' wife and bairnies three.'

> 'Gae seek your succour at Branksmone Ha',
> For succour ye'se get nane frae me,
> Gae seek yer succour where ye paid blackmail,
> For, man! ye ner paid money tae me.'

Scotland's rulers tried in vain to curb these Borderers' activities; expeditions hanged, drowned in Teviot or carted off to

Edinburgh for trial and execution various ringleaders all to no avail. Once the avenging force had departed into the Lothians little time was spent in mourning those who had suffered the ultimate punishment and the old trade, cattle stealing being far from a dishonourable profession at least in the eyes of the participants, was soon resumed.

Elsewhere the reiving activities met less sympathy. Gavin Dunbar, the Archbishop of Glasgow, issued against them, a 'monition of curses' fifteen hundred words long and published throughout the Border country. Dunbar cursed in the long list, the heads, the hairs on their heads, nose, tongue, in fact from the top of the head to the soles of their feet. He cursed them coming, going, indoors, outdoors; he cursed their equipment down to ploughs and harrows. In fact it was one of the most comprehensive cursings of all time which seems to have had little effect upon the men of the Border marches.

Looking back from the comfort of the late twentieth century we cannot imagine the kind of life led by the Borderers of the sixteenth. We have the ballads and written records, the latter mainly from English sources. Who is to say that these accounts are accurate; the writers and recorders would be as susceptible to the foibles and prejudices of human nature as we are today.

It would be easy to condemn the reivers' activities when set against present day standards, but these were violent times and survival far from easy in the high reaches of the Border valleys. What must not be forgotten is that during the sixteenth century the Scottish Marches were subject to recurring major raids, not merely by Northumberland or Cumberland families, but by English armies. Time and time again the valleys next to the Border were harassed, robbed and left in smoking ruins, leaving little choice for the people who lived there but to sally out by night in an attempt to put something back in store against the hard winter months.

Doubtless life was difficult, declared as outlaws and harried by their sovereigns, who can blame the march men for lifting a few sheep and cattle.

The Middle March retains more evidence of the clan names which bound the Border families together than is found in the Eastern. Turning to such a humble publication as B.T. Borders Directory there are few entries under the principal families of

Home, Swinton and Trotter in the Merse. Yet in that part of the Borders dealt with in this book the Armstrongs remain, although few; the Elliots and the Douglases are well represented and the Scotts numerous, around their old clan areas.

Along the valleys, and in the mill towns the guid Border tongue can still be heard. Upper Teviotdale and Hawick once had a unique accent, shared to some extent, but softer in pronunciation, with Liddesdale and Eskdale in Dumfriesshire; again it may yet be heard and appreciated but for how long. Walter Elliot of Selkirk, an able exponent of the guid Borders' tongue laments its decline in verse in 'The Borders tongue':

> Ah mind awfy weel in ma younger days,
> When the tongue they spoke on the Ettrick's braes,
> Or the Yarrae hills was sae crisp an' clear,
> Gi'ed a lift tae the hert an' a joy tae the ear.

> Noo in the valleys ye hear tongues o' Wales,
> London, New York an' the Yorkshire dales,
> The auld valley folk are aa wede awa,
> Ye scarcely can meet wi a native at aa.

> Ma guid Border Scots is considered uncouth
> As folk try tae speak wi a bool in their mooth.
> Ah'll sin be a ghost in me ain native land,
> An' speak wi a tongue that few understand.

It may cheer Walter up to know that by far the majority of people spoken to by myself while compiling both this, and the previous book, by far the majority spoke guid Border Scots. So hopefully the local accents and dialects will prevail despite the influence of the dreaded imported soap operas and hopefully the incomers will soon be converted to native speakers.

Returning to the earlier Borderers however, it is not surprising to find that these freebooters preferred some form of fortification as a dwelling house; pele or peel towers dot the hill valleys. Perhaps many of these date from the decree issued following the battle of Flodden that every man owning property over £100 value had to build a peel or defensive building upon his property. Many of these must have existed in the Borders prior to there being a legal obligation for their construction. These towers can be found in an equal abundance in valleys such as Yarrow and Manor, both of these much further from the Border than those of Teviot and Liddel.

For the main part the simple square tower was not built to withstand an extensive siege. Few instances are recorded of a raiding party as opposed to an invading army mounting a concentrated attack upon these crude fortresses where living conditions must have been extremely cramped. In various states of preservation from heaps of stones to desirable dwellings, these towers remain among the Border valleys to this day. Many, especially those in Liddesdale belonging to the Armstrongs, were flung down following the Union of the Crowns; others elsewhere remain habitable while some have recently been restored.

Castles proper are few in this part of the world; that of Peebles lies below the parish church while Selkirk's Royal Castle is but a green mound. Hermitage is the major fortress but others such as Newark Tower on Yarrow played their part in Border history. Perhaps the best preserved small castle is that of Neidpath, overlooking the Tweed on a commanding site above Peebles. Neidpath is everything a castle should be.

What must be borne in mind is that the horseback festivals in this part of the Borders have nothing to do with celebrating the exploits of sixteenth-century cattle thieves. The two oldest events, the Common Ridings of Hawick and Selkirk, are, as the name suggests, a ceremonial tour of the town's common land boundaries, once an important practical task to ensure there had been no infringement upon the burgh land by neighbours. Others of the one-time burgh festivals are of more recent origin, which does not mean that towns holding these did not at one time have a practical 'Common Riding'.

Festivals emphasise local pride, a powerful emotion here, hence the stories of Borderers stuck in adverse conditions, be it blizzards or battlefields, turning to their companion from the same town with a quote, 'Aye Jock, it's bad enough here, but mind you it could hae been a hale lot worse, we could jist as easy have been stuck in Galashiels,' or whatever the rival town, 'for the day'; or the Selkirk man who 'would rather be a lamppost in Selkirk than the provost o' Gala'.

At local festivals can be seen and heard one of the less well-known features of Borders culture, the brass and silver bands which add their own special brand of music to these and other occasions. Brass and silver bands are associated with that other centre of the wool trade in Yorkshire, where they enjoyed the sponsorship of the mill owners. Here in the Borders the bands are independent of outside help, being entirely supported by the local community. Judging by the number of young musicians in these bands their future is secure and their music is set to echo through the Borders for some time to come.

Warlike sounds may still be heard throughout the Borders on most winter Saturdays as teams from rival towns battle for possession of the oval ball; this is firmly rugby country — not, it must be said, that rugby is played to the exclusion of the other game where a bag of wind encased in a leather cover is booted around a field. Soccer also has its adherents on the haughs alongside Tweed and Teviot. Skills may not rival those in first division football, but who can compete where the names of the teams are concerned. Glasgow Rangers or Dundee United sound dull when compared to Gala Fairydene or Hawick Royal Albert; Hearts of Midlothian are in with a chance but, after all, that does have a Border connection.

Not unnaturally in a land of so many rivers angling is a popular pastime for locals and visitors. Salmon angling remains good on the Tweed itself upstream to Peebles and beyond. Mainly an autumn fishery when backend fish run, success on the upper beats is dependent upon high rainfall and plenty of water to encourage fish to forge quickly upstream in a fresh condition. Autumn fish soon become discoloured as they don their spawning livery of black in the case of males and red in females.

Ettrick has improved as salmon river, appearing to have a better share of spring run fish than previously, or is it a case that with the increased demand for salmon angling little fished waters are becoming more exploited? Salmon angling is less expensive on the upper beats than the lower prime reaches, being well within the means of most anglers with a desire to catch salar the leaper. A high incidence of sniggling or foul hooking, i.e., deliberately hooking a salmon without the fish co-operating by taking the fly in its mouth, has led to restrictions on type of fly and weight of flyline being introduced on the upper river.

Remains of Dryhope Tower in Yarrow; cauld comfort and a degree of safety for its inhabitants in past times.

Poaching in this part of the world was for long undertaken by the 'blacksmiths fly', otherwise the gaff or cleek, used in conjunction with a torch on the feeder streams at night. Before the many weirs or caulds used by the mills were removed, the method of poaching was described as, 'running the cauld'. This meant waiting on one side until a salmon was seen struggling up through the thin water spilling over the lip where the operative or poacher would sprint across the treacherous slippery surface, cleeking the fish in the passing, then onward to the opposite bank.

Trout angling is perhaps the mainstay of sport for most Borderers. The quality of trouting here is first class, their capture sometimes a difficult matter. Fish of over three pounds are regularly recorded from the waters of the many angling associations who control most of the trout fishing in the Borders. Here, more so than in the east, there is a choice of running or still waters for the angler to cast his line upon. The two major natural lochs in the Borders, St Mary's and the Loch of the Lowes are found in the upper valley of the Yarrow.

These are augmented by a number of artificial waters in the shape of reservoirs — Talla, Megget and Fruid being the largest — pumping their water to the Lothians, where hopefully the citizens appreciate the clean soft water from the Borders. Smaller reservoirs provide local water supplies while there can still be found a number of dams built to store a supply of water for millpower. Most stillwaters, whether natural or artificial, contain a head of brown or rainbow trout stocked for sporting purposes; others contain pike and other coarse fish providing sport for the truly dedicated during the winter months when trout and salmon angling is closed.

Control of the Tweed and its tributaries is vested in the River Tweed Commissioners who have a bailliff force extending throughout the entire river system. Pollution problems are dealt with by the River Tweed Purification Board who have their headquarters in Melrose while the Tweed Foundation, a registered charity, works towards the general improvement of the river habitat.

Outdoor sporting activities are well served in this part of the world; the old roads crossing from valley to valley make superb mountain bike routes without damaging the fragile heath. Hill walking, while it may not have the challenge of the Highlands or the crowds of the English Lake District, has an appeal of its own. There are few 'honeypots' to draw in crowds; among the vast acres of hill and moor the gangrel can wander day long with scarce another human encounter.

Professional instruction is available here for a number of sports; naturally angling ranks among them, but one can learn the ancient sport of hawking, get to grips with a mountain bike or discover some of the intricacies of sheepdog handling.

Golf can be enjoyed at a reasonable cost from most Border towns, where as in the case of Hawick the 18-hole course occupies part of the old Burgh Common Lands on Vertish Hill. An athletics stadium is sited at Tweedbank near Galashiels, while all the major towns dealt with in this book have swimming pools and in some instances indoor sports facilities such as Hawick's Teviotdale Leisure Centre.

Main roads are just that in this part of the world. The hustle of the motorway is none existent; even dual carriageway stretches are few and far between. The A68 forms the principal

Hillwalkers on Ruberslaw. The view is superb.

route here carrying traffic north and south through the heart
of the Borders. Perhaps the 'best' road where motor traffic is
concerned (east–west routes are less suitable) the A7 from
Hawick into Dumfries, despite its trunk title, is little more than
a country road, a description suitable also for the Selkirk–Moffat
road winding its way up Yarrow and around St Mary's Loch.
Alongside the Gala Water the A7(T), after diverse deviations
from Hawick by Selkirk and Galashiels, forms an alternative
route into the Lothians when the A68 is impassable with snow
at Soutra Hill, a regular winter occurrence.

Peebles is surprisingly close to Edinburgh, reached by the
A703 up Eddleston Water by way of Leadburn. What this part
of the Borders offers the pleasure motorist are the many miles
of B and unclassified roads. With some planning these can offer
alternatives to the busier main roads — seek the brown or even
the yellow roads on the O.S. Landranger maps. These are roads
which lead deep into the hills, leapfrogging from valley to valley,
where for the driver the biggest hazards are the hill sheep who
prefer to lie sometimes on the warm tarmac road rather than
the damp grass or heather.

Roads, of any kind, were only being constructed throughout
the Borders late in the eighteenth century. Sir Walter Scott is
said to have caused a stir when visiting Liddesdale in the first
wheeled conveyance ever to have been seen in that valley.

Agriculture improvement took place from 1750 onwards when it was realised that much better crops could be raised with the use of lime. Roads passable by cart rather than packhorse were necessary to bring this important ingredient from the Lothians or Northumberland. Ironically there was little or no lime or coal in this part of the Borders where its use was of the utmost importance, although pits of shell marl were exploited as fertiliser which had a similar, if somewhat weaker, effect to burnt lime on the land.

Simultaneously with agricultural improvement, this was a time of industrial expansion in the woollen industry with coal being used more and more both as a domestic and industrial fuel. Wealthy 'gentlemen' seeing the need for improved transport, or perhaps sniffing a profit in the offing, subscribed to the building of many roads throughout the Borders. Some remain the basis of motor transport to this day.

Once the iron road of the railway companies reached distant parts, it brought cheaper coal in particular to the mill towns. Coal was essential for the steam engines, which had replaced the earlier water-powered spinning and weaving machinery, and as the industry expanded, for the dying of yarn and finally drying of finished cloth. Rates paid for coal in Galashiels, for instance, fell from 28s to 16s a ton with the arrival of the railway in 1849. Reaching into river valleys, crossing bleak moorland it is hard to believe now as nature and development take over the trackbeds, yards and stations that rail transport was for a brief period the prime mover of goods and people in the Borders.

Education falls under the jurisdiction of the Borders Regional Council in primary schools spread throughout the rural areas and high schools at main centres of population. The Borders College provides further education from a base in Galashiels offering a range of subjects covering all aspects of manufacturing and service industries in the Borders. Appropriately, 'The Scottish College of Textiles', now part of Heriot-Watt University, Edinburgh, is found at Galashiels.

Sharing the same boundaries as the Borders Regional Council the local enterprise company, Scottish Borders Enterprise, is dedicated to the promotion business within the Region. It is a broad challenge with traditional industries in severe difficulties, unemployment rising and many young people forced to leave the Region in search of employment.

What the future holds for the old industries of the Borders is impossible to foresee without the benefit of a crystal ball, though electronics are now well established in Selkirk and Galashiels. New enterprises have arisen, some utilising the old textile mills, others in purpose-built units. Businesses as diverse as the manufacture of glass paper weights, high class leather clothing and stained glass windows are but a few which have arisen in recent years.

Tourism may be the answer to replace the jobs now no longer available in textiles, despite the fact that many Borderers are reluctant to work in this industry. Compact in comparison to the Highlands, the Borders could never absorb the same amount of visitors as the former without the destruction of the very thing they had come to see.

Constantly, individuals, the Regional and District Councils and Scottish Borders Enterprise are striving to bring new business and employment to the Scottish Borders.

# CHAPTER 2

## *Teviotdale*

Teviotdale in former times was part of Scotland's Middle March. The perimeter of what was the county of Roxburgh through which Teviot runs is set right against the English border. One of the largest of Tweed's tributaries joining the Tweed at Kelso, Teviot in turn receives the water of several major and minor streams, principal among these being the Borthwick, Slitrig, Rule, Ale, Jed and Kale. Some of these streams were dealt with in *Borders 1*, from Kelso to Jedfoot; of the others, many have a tale to tell of more turbulent times along the Border.

Aided by their neighbours in nearby Liddesdale, the families of Kerr, Scott and Douglas kept the pot boiling in Teviotdale, which when seasoned with a sprinkling of Elliots, Turnbulls and Armstrongs makes a sure recipe for a hot dish. Already, in *Discovering the Borders 1*, we have looked at the lower part of Teviot around Roxburgh Castle where the landscape is virtually the same as that of the Merse. Indeed it is not until upstream of where the Jed joins Teviot, near Monteviot House, that the uplands become apparent from the banks.

Entering Teviotdale by the Jedburgh–Hawick road, Minto Crags are one of the most prominent features on the north bank, crowned by Fatlips Castle which is of fairly recent vintage, constructed from the ruins of an earlier sixteenth-century tower in 1857. Built as a museum for artifacts collected worldwide by the Elliots of Minto, the present day tower is in danger of following the fate of its predecessor.

The Elliot name is still prevalent in Teviotdale, and nearby Liddesdale, where the family arrived from Angus in the early part of the fourteenth century when they were granted land in both valleys by Robert the Bruce. During the Scottish struggle for independence this was dangerous country; doubtless the Bruce brought the Elliots here to strengthen his southern defences.

Several spellings of the name exist, often recorded in the past as Elvate. A doggerel verse on where the different name spell-

26

ings belong has little association with the homes of different branches of the family today:

Double L and single T,
Elliots of Minto and Wolflee.

Single T and single L,
The Eliots they in Stobs that dwell.

Single L and double T,
Eliotts of St Germains be.

But double L and double T,
The De'il may ken wha they may be.

Today these spelling variations and the houses of their origin can only be regarded as a jingle. The majority of Elliots listed in the Borders' telephone directory come under the above spelling. Single L and single T are not listed, while the late Lady Frances Eliott of Stobs, one of the best loved and most forthright characters in this part of the world, should, according to the jingle, have only a single T spelling. By far the majority of the double L and double T Elliotts are found outwith the valleys of Liddle and Teviot.

Minto House was the birthplace of Jean Elliot who wrote one version of *Flowers o' the Forest*. Unlike that by Mrs Cockburn of Fairnielee, Jean's version was a lament for Flodden written over four hundred years after the event.

As discussed elsewhere in this book Elliots in one form of the name or another have played a major part in Border affairs down through the centuries. The present Lord Minto, an Elliot, continuess this trait as independent councillor for Hermitage ward since the region was set up in 1974. He was elected Convener in 1990.

Barnhill's Bed, said to be the haunt of the notorious outlaw, occupies a ledge on the Crags and is mentioned in Scott's fictitious work, *The Lay of the Last Minstrel*.

> On Minto Crags the moonbeams glint,
> Where Barnhill hewed his bed of flint,
> Who flung his outlaw'd limbs to rest,
> Where falcons hang their giddy nest.

Lying north of Minto towards Selkirk the Ale Water traces a parallel course to that of Teviot, but must run a few miles yet before the waters can join. A cluster of villages are found above the Ale Water; Midlem both by name and situation with its triangular village green of Anglian origin was mentioned in the Charter for Selkirk Abbey in 1119.

Lilliesleaf on the other hand is one straight street, but it has its backrows, also a feature of Anglian settlements. While the present church at Lilliesleaf dates from 1771, with later extensions, the original church which was in the diocese of the Archbishop of Glasgow dates from 1110 AD. The original building, itself replaced in 1430, is said to have stood on the site now occupied by the burial aisles of the Riddells of Riddell and of Muselie, and that of the Stewarts of Hermiston. The church at Lilliesleaf boasts one of the oldest christening fonts in the south of Scotland, in fact from the original 1110 kirk, although the font may be from later that century. It lay for many, perhaps hundreds of years at the site of the old kirk, in what is described as a moss. Retrieved in 1883 when extensive renovations were carried out to the building, the font now stands in the 1910 apse. Nearby is a tiny child's stone coffin, almost toy-like but a poignant artifact. Did, one wonders, the infant who was interred in the coffin receive its baptism in the stone font?

Opposite Minto Hills on Teviot's south bank, the Rule Water joins with Teviot; three miles upstream Bedrule was the centre of one of the most troublesome of Border clans, the Turnbulls. Like other valleys within Teviotdale, that of Rule Water saw its share of devastation from over the Border. Without a doubt the Turnbulls and their allies in turn wrought equal havoc upon the English valleys of Rede and Tyne.

Turnbull, Trummel or Trumbel, as the name is still occasionally known in the Borders, is said to originate from an incident at Callander when Robert Bruce was in danger of being gored by a wild bull. Whether William of Rule was the first Turn-e-bull, who wrestled the enraged beast to the ground, is not known.

Perhaps like Scott of Buccleuch the origins of the name form the basis of a good story.

Turnbulls fought with the English at the start of the Battle of Ancrum Moor, but upon seeing the day going in favour of the Scots, turned upon their former allies and assisted in the final rout. A Turnbull said to be a giant of a man was killed in single combat prior to the Battle of Hallidon Hill near Berwick in 1333, at the Redeswire Fray, 'Auld Bedroule' wi' aw the Turnbulls at his back seems to have played a prominent part in the proceedings. However they seem to have been a thorn in the flesh of the Scottish monarchy in the sixteenth century as in 1510 James IV led an expedition against the clan. Bearing naked swords and wearing rope halters two hundred Turnbulls met the royal force, the latter being conveniently placed to mete out the usual Stewart justice to the Borderers. One must have been less troublesome than others as William Turnbull of Bedrule as Bishop of Glasgow was responsible for founding the city's university in 1451. A plaque within Bedrule Kirk commemorates both man and event.

The Rule Water is a secretive river where the motorist is concerned — its lower course at least hidden from the road, where it passes a large motte hill, one of the several remains of fortifications in the valley, spanning the era from the iron-age Celts up to the medieval tower. There is nothing secretive, however, about Bedrule kirk standing on a prominent knoll overlooking the Rule Water. Enlarged in 1914, the building features within the armonial bearings of many of the Border families who have owned the land alongside Rule Water over the centuries.

East from the Rule Valley lies the village of Chesters with its three kirks. The ancient Souden Kirk was excavated in 1910 and the partly restored tower dedicated in memory of the Battle of Otterburn. A second church lies roofless in the village while the newer building lies a little distance outwith the settlement. This among other things features what is described as a *super-altar* stone bearing five finely inscribed crosses set into the 1914–18 war memorial Communion table. Discovered during the 1910 Souden excavations by the Hawick Archaeological Society, other carved stones from the building are preserved on the site beside the A6088.

At Southdean the ancient hill crossing route known as the Wheel Causeway descends to beside the Jed Water from the Cheviot Ridge. The route is said to date from prehistory but among the more recent users have been Charles Edward Stuart and Edward I, the latter on one of his many missions to hammer the Scots.

Returning to the Rule Water, Bonchester Bridge with its hotels and camp site is the principal settlement on the Rule today. Four roads meet in or near the village below Bonchester Hill crowned with its fort and settlement. One of these, the B6375, is the back road into Liddesdale, by Note o the Gate to Saughtree where, by turning south, Kielder Water is but over the next brow. Much of the B6375 now passes through the centre of Wauchope Forest, itself part of the Borders Forest Park where the Forestry Commission have provided a picnic place overlooking the Hyndlee Burn.

We have seen and may see elsewhere in this book that the Borders was a favourite haunt for Scottish Kings and Queens from earliest times. Here the Stewarts and their predecessors sported with hound and horse in pursuit of roe and red deer, or with hawk in search of muirfowl and hill game. Fitting it is,

Old Kirk, Southdean.

therefore, that near Bonchester Bridge the Durman-Walters, Diana and Len, run the Scottish Academy of Falconry.

To the layman it would seem an almost impossible task to train a free flying bird to hunt and return to hand. In fact it takes about six weeks with around a patient daily half an hour on each bird. The secret in flying falcons lies in the feeding; birds being flown are weighed daily to check that they are at their best flying weight and fed accordingly. A bird too well fed will be reluctant to hunt, and perhaps equally reluctant to return to the falconer when enticed by a titbit of food. It is a fascinating sight to see raptors flying free (especially our own peregrine, one of the species known in hawking terms as a longwing), the high dive or stoop to the prey, the rush of air past the fixed wings guiding the bird to its target.

Birds of prey — the peregrine, goshawk or the tiny merlin — are the principal native species of hawks flown by the Academy and are reared by the Durman-Walter's. In fact the Scottish Academy was the first establishment in this country to produce a goshawk by artificial insemination. Today this is the only method to procure birds of prey for falconry as the taking of young from nests or eyries is now forbidden by law.

The six-day courses run by the Scottish Academy of Falconry can be residential if required and range from Introductory through to Advanced Hawking and the Goshawk Spectacular, and to the ultimate Grouse Hawking on Scottish Moors. Both Diana and Len have contributed material to magazines, radio and television on falconry while the Academy's displays at local fairs never fail to impress the onlooker.

Likened to a crouching lion when viewed from east or west, one thing difficult to ignore around the Rule Water is the bulk of volcanic Rubers Law overlooking the village of Denholm. Early fortifications can be found on the summit where bronze-age remains were unearthed; its prominence used in later years as a Roman signal station, then by Covenanters who utilised a flat rock as their Communion table.

Without doubt in this second book on the Borders, the view from Ruberslaw thrust almost into the heart of Teviotdale is unsurpassed. Nor does it take a mountaineer to gain the summit — anything from an hour to an hour and a half from the village of Denholm will gain the top. The way lies around the workings of an old sandstone quarry; the track entrance is easily recognised by the old green painted iron summer seat which appears to be a permanent feature. Once past the quarry, which is in no way dangerous, walk around field margins, through a gate where a pond will be seen on the right, then uphill alongside a wood to gain the moorland area of heather and in late summer delicious sweet blaeberries.

A stunted patch of Scots firs can be passed on the right where a four-wheel-drive vehicle track leads to the top with its O.S. triangulation point. Look now east, beyond Pienel Heugh to the bowl of the Merse, beyond in the low ground Tweed empties into the North Sea. Swing around to the south and the hulk of Cheviot, then the Border Ridge, along the skyline by Carter Bar and the Wauchope Forest. West lies the Maiden Paps, then around the compass to the uplands of Ettrick, Yarrow and Tweed with the blue line of the Lammermuirs to the north. Here indeed you have the Borders at your feet.

Denholm is, of course, the birthplace in 1775 of Dr John Leyden, one of the greatest linguists of all time who died in Bativia, Java in 1811. In his short life of 36 years, Leyden, the son of a shepherd, completed training as both a minister and doctor, became proficient in over forty languages and as a contemporary of Sir Walter Scott was instrumental in collecting much of the material for Scott's *Minstrelsy* and was a considerable poet in his own right.

Despite his knowledge of other languages John Leyden never lost his strong Teviotdale accent, having been told while in India to 'mend his English'. This he refused to do as he considered that what others believed to be the proper use of this language would spoil his native Scots. Never one to comply with the rules of society Leyden is said to have surprised Scott and his guests after dinner, his approach like the sound of a rising tempest. A fragment of an old ballad had been discovered by Scott, but diligent search threw no light upon it in its entirety. Leyden, however, knew of a source and set off to walk fifty miles to obtain the remnants and recited it over and over again on his return journey, right into Scott's drawing room.

With only a rudimentary early education John Leyden was encouraged by the local minister, beginning his higher education, as was customary for the time for a lad of his station, by

Stunted Pines on ruberslaw.

Leyden's birthplace at Denholm.

setting out to Edinburgh with little more than a sack of meal
to keep body and soul together. Originally Leyden qualified as
a minister but later changed course to qualify in six months in
medicine and surgery, setting out for India in 1803 to take up
a post as assistant surgeon in Madras. Here Leyden became
proficient in Asian languages, so much so that by 1805 he was
professor of Hindustani in Calcutta. By 1811 he was off on an
expedition to Java with Lord Minto where unfortunately the
brilliant career was cut short when Leyden caught a fatal fever.

Central in Denholm's extensive village green is the ornate
monument erected in 1861 to honour the Doctor. Restoration
was carried out by Denholm Community Council in 1982 and
among the fundraising activities was a sponsored walk to Edinburgh by young people of Denholm who following the route
taken by Leyden when he went to university.

A quotation from Leyden's 'Scenes of Infancy' can be found
on the memorial.

> Dear native valleys may you long retain,
> The charter freedom of mountain swain,
> Long may your sounding glades in union sweet,
> May rural innocence and beauty meet,
> And still be duly heard at twilight calm,
> From every cot the peasant's chanted psalm.

The house where Leyden was born stands on the north side
of the green, one of the few thatched houses found in this part
of the Borders, while a simple pillar marks the site of
Henlawshiel below Ruberslaw, where at the age of one John's
parents removed to the cottage once situated here on his grand
uncle's farm at Nether Tofts.

As if one famous son was not enough in the linguistic field
Denholm has a second in the shape of Sir James A. H. Murray,
who began his working life at the age of twelve herding cows
for a half-yearly wage of twelve shillings, a working life which
ended in 1915 as editor of the *New English Dictionary*.

By Hawick, 'The Auld Grey Toon', Teviotdale has changed
into a real upland valley pushing the town out and upwards
away from the river side. The original settlement of Hawick —
the hedged town — is thought to have been by Anglo-Saxon
tribes around the junction of the Slitrig and Teviot sometime

in the seventh century. About the same time St Cuthbert built a chapel on the present site of St Mary's Church.

In the twelfth century the Normans arrived with the French family of Lovels establishing a wooden castle on the Motte. What life was like in one of these timber forts is difficult to imagine. Certainly there could be little in the way of comfort within the Hawick version as it measures a bare fifteen yards in diameter on its summit. Once thought to be much older, dating to pre-dark-age times, oak sprigs are still worn at the Common Riding, marking the once popular view of a druidical connection.

Later the Lovels built a more substantial tower at Drumlanrig beside the Slitrig. This in turn was replaced by the Black Tower of Drumlanrig, on the same site now incorporated in the Tower Hotel which at the time of writing is subject to extensive renovation from its previous semiderelict state. Drumlanrig was the Hawick residence of, first, the Douglas family and then the Scotts of Buccleugh. It was by a charter granted by James Douglas on October 11th 1537 that Hawick was created a Burgh of Barony. This status was held along with its associated civic pride right up until 1975, when the reorganisation of local government swept away provosts and town councils with the stroke of a pen — what centuries of cross-border conflicts had failed to achieve.

Pride in native towns is fierce throughout the Borders; in the 'Teries', as those born in Hawick are called, this pride runs even stronger than elsewhere. Teries derives from the Hawick Common riding song, its origins lost in the past but thought to be a plea to the pagan Norse Gods — Thor and Odin. 'Teribus, ye Teri Odin', meaning 'Thor be with us, both Thor and Odin'.

> Scotia felt thine ire, O Odin!
> On the bloody field of Flodden;
> There our fathers fell with honour,
> Round their King and country's banner.
> *Chorus*
> Teribus ye teri odin,
> Sons of heroes slain at Flodden,
> Imitating Border bowmen
> Aye defend your rights and Common.

The Hawick Horse.

This slogan is incorporated into the arms of the Community of Hawick, which also honour the Douglas killed in Spain taking Robert the Bruce's heart on the crusades, and into a blue and gold flag in honour of 1514.

To find out why 1514 is so important to Hawick see the monument on the east end of the High Street known as 'The Horse', a fine bronze monument showing a young man mounted on horseback bearing aloft a flag. This depicts an incident in 1514, when Scotland was in a much weakened state following the Battle of Flodden fought the preceding year.

In the year following Flodden, English forces were busy raiding in the Scottish Borders, a kind of self-service free-for-all, with even a party from Hexham Priory out in search of bounty. At Hornshole, two miles downstream from Hawick, a band of youths from the town surprised these raiders at daybreak where in the ensuing skirmish the English seem to have come off second best, suffering the ignominy of having their banner captured.

This was the original of the banner blue carried by the Hawick Cornet in the Common Riding celebrations held each year in June. Now replaced by a replica in the proceedings, Hawick has long since made peace with the Hexham Priory and has gifted a further replica banner to hang in the nave there.

Hawick Common Riding reaches a climax on the Friday and Saturday following the first Monday in June, although events have been leading in this direction for some time. Two weeks before the Common Riding one of the most gruelling rides in

Hawick Cornet leaving Tower Hotel yard during the Common Riding celebrations.

the Borders Festivals takes place over the hills to Mosspaul Hotel, on the watershed between Teviot and Ewes Water in Dumfries. Those who complete the course qualify for the badge of the, 'Ancient Order of Mosstroopers' which, like all Hawick rideouts, is restricted to males only.

Thursday evening, 'the nicht afore the morn' in a colour bussing ceremony when at least one of the fairer sex has a chance to participate when the Cornet's Lass 'busses' the town standard with blue and gold ribbons. Otherwise it's a men-only affair in the main events; even when the civic leader happens to be a woman the customary invitation to official functions for the equivalent of Provost of Hawick is not forthcoming.

Once the banner blue is handed to the Cornet he is charged by the Chief Magistrate to, 'ride the marches of the Commonty of Hawick according to custom' and return the Flag, 'unstained and unsullied' on completion. An announcement warns all burgesses of Hawick to gather in their best apparel the following day to attend the Cornet in his duties. A foot parade through Hawick led by Saxhorn and Drum and Fife band culminates in the Cornet bussing the flag on the horse statue honouring the deeds of the Hawick youth of 1514 at Hornshole.

Six a.m. on Common Riding Friday in Hawick is not a time nor place for those who like to lie a bed as the Drum and Fife band parades the streets wakening all citizens to their duties. Before these can take place there is 'The Snuffin'' a ceremonial distribution of snuff near the site of Hawick's Auld Brig. A ceremony which is said to date from the time when the taking of snuff was a regular habit, it was also considered sociable to offer a pinch to friends when meeting, or to pass round the snuff at any form of gathering. Hawick's Auld Brig was so narrow it was virtually impossible for one Teri to pass another here without the pouch being proffered.

The boundary riding itself, once essential to make sure no neighbouring landowners were making any encroachment upon the Common Land, is symbolic in the cutting of a turf. Prior to this the principals have enjoyed a refreshment of curds and cream at St Leonard's Farm before the Cornet leads the cavalcade to Hawick Moor for an afternoon of horse racing.

Horse races, the singing of Teribus or the Auld Refrain as it is known, a ceremonial dipping of the Flag in Teviot and an all-night ball lasting until daylight the next morning, when the Cornet and his party greet the dawn from the Mote all take place. Overnight the Flag has been on display from the town hall balcony until Saturday it is paraded through the town prior to another session of horse racing before being handed back, 'unstained and unsullied', meaning mainly that the bearer has been by his conduct and behaviour a credit to Hawick. Somehow it would seem unthinkable that any Cornet would ever deem to be otherwise.

Conflict with the English ceased in the seventeenth century as Teviotdale settled down to a peaceful existence of wool growing and textile production. Yet the people of Hawick were still willing to stand up for what they knew to be right and proper as exemplified by some of the ongauns following the Reform Act of 1832.

To counteract the Liberal following in the district, Tory supporters were buying up small parcels of land around Hawick, giving them as owners the right to vote for a parliamentary candidate in that constituency. Hawick's townsfolk, among others, had supported the Act although it was not until 1868 that further legislation gave all males the vote. However back in 1832 when Edinburgh citizens were 'bussed' or rather carriaged into Hawick to vote for their Tory candidate, many never reached the polling places. A dip in Teviot's cold waters after being dragged from their conveyances by determined Teries, was the reward for their insolence.

Woollens and the Borders go hand-in-hand. A trade which, as stated elsewhere, dates back to the twelfth century and the founding of the Border abbeys when 'Forest Wool' was exported for the use of Flemish weavers through the port of Berwick-upon-Tweed. Throughout Britain even in the sixteenth century the importance of the native woollen industry was recognised, an English Act of 1571 decreeing that all persons over six years of age were required to wear woollen caps on Sundays and holidays.

In Scotland one of the earliest products of the hand knitters was the woollen cap, the 'blue bonnet', especially famous in the Borders. While other Border towns wove, Hawick's textile industry was based on knitting. Large scale manufacture of knitted clothing first came to the town in 1722 when Bailie John Hardie established a business at 37 High Street producing machine knitted hose. These stockings replaced earlier styles which were formed by sewing, making an uncomfortable seam between the wearer's foot and boot. First linen, then a mixture of linen and worsted was used, later to be converted entirely to wool, although the original output from Bailie Hardie's small works was some 2,500 pairs per year.

Almost a hundred years later in 1816, Hawick had 510 knitting frames in operation producing 328,000 pairs a year. Piecework must have been the normal practice in those times as in 1817 the employers decided to reduce the price paid to their workers by 6d a dozen. Strikes resulted, dragging on for many months with the leaders, including one James Hogg — said to be the author of Teribus — suffering terms of imprisonment.

The earlier knitted garments made in Hawick were underwear, your combinations, long johns and woolly vest. When earlier this century it became the custom to wear knitted clothing as an outer layer the way was open for the makers of the humble vest to branch out into new fashionable products.

Hawick has gone on from these simple beginnings to be the leading town in the knitwear industry; once it was said that mid-week, with so many young women from the Borders staying in Hawick, females outnumbered males at a ratio of 3 to 1. Many world famous names in the knitwear industry can be found in Hawick, firms which are leaders in fashion and technology. Some of these continue to thrive, mainly by the excellence of their product, since now in the early 1990s recession has bit deep into this Border's industry. Despite this downturn Hawick remains the knitwear capital of Scotland where with a population of 17,000, 60 per cent of those working are involved in the knitwear industry.

The full story of Hawick's woollen industry is told in the town's museum at Wilton Park Lodge on the north bank of the Teviot. Here also is an account of Hawick past in a series of exhibits including artifacts from Harden House on Borthwick Water, home of 'Auld Wat' a famous local reiver.

Jimmie Guthrie, motor cycle racing champion, is also remembered at Wilton Lodge in newspaper clippings recording his success which included six wins in the Isle of Man Tourist

Trophy Championships. Jimmie was killed while taking part in the 1937 German Grand Prix when it is said he swerved to avoid someone walking on the track and sustained fatal injuries in the resulting crash. A bronze memorial in Wilton Lodge grounds, one of three erected after his death by subscriptions from motor cycle enthusiasts worldwide, records the achievements of one who was really a local hero. Older inhabitants of Hawick recall Jimmie practising his survival technique in Wilton Park, rolling off his machine with his head tucked in to avoid injury, which in the event of emergency failed to save his life.

A famous modern day son of Hawick can be found in yachtsman Chay Blyth who first sprang to fame in his Atlantic rowing excursion with John Ridgeway. Chay received the freedom of Hawick in 1973 in recognition of his exploits which were then only beginning.

For their Sunday afternoon stroll Hawick residents are faced with a dilemma, not in where they may walk but which walk to select — the grounds of Wilton Park being only one of many Teviot-side strolls which can be enjoyed by residents and visitors alike. Wilton Lodge Park with a total of 107 acres must be one of the best and incorporates a number of recreational areas including playing fields, tennis courts, bowling and putting greens. The Wilton grounds came to Hawick through a series of owners, beginning with the Langland family in the thirteenth century, through Elliots, Andersons and Pringles until purchased by the town in 1889 for housing purposes and industrial development.

Neither of these uses was necessary at the time and Wilton Park was retained as a unique amenity, where in addition to the Guthrie Statue, are memorials to Hawick's sons who died in the Boer War and both World Wars. The remains of the old Mercat Cross are also retained near the museum, close by which can be found a scented garden for the pleasure of the visually handicapped beside a waterfall on the Cala Burn or Wilton Dean.

Mansfield Park on the other hand is the home of Hawick Rugby Club and is known simply as, 'The Greens', here in contrast to the 'Auld Grey Toon' title of the rugby song which proclaims Hawick as 'Queen o aw the Borders'.

What though her lads are a wild wee,
And ill tae keep good order,
'Mang ither toons she bears the gree,
Hawick's Queen o' a' the Border.

Rugby first came to Hawick in 1872 with the club obtaining the present site in 1888. Something like religious fervour is attached to the oval ball game in the town with apparently every spare acre of level ground near Hawick sprouting the tall goalposts familiar with the game.

Nearby at Mansfield Haugh is the home of Hawick Royal Albert. The soccer club was founded in 1946 and despite the dominance of rugby in the Borders, retains a staunch following in their matches in the East of Scotland League.

Hawick Golf Club boasts an eighteen-hole course, on what was once common land belonging to the old burgh on Vertish Hill to the south west of the town, and claims to be the oldest course in the Borders. Angling is well catered for with not only Teviot and its many local tributaries but a ring of natural and artificial hill lochs providing sport for both the game and coarse fisherman.

Upstream from Hawick as the Teviot and A7 thread their way westwards Teviotdale assumes a truly upland appearance as the hills press in upon the infant river. Along the verges of the valleys the hills have been well settled in; forts, settlements and standing stones are abundant while the Catrail, an ancient earthwork, carves its way across the countryside. Towers and castles of a more recent era are found nearer the river valleys, well known in some cases by the deeds of their past owners and their mention in ballad and poem.

Overlooking the A7 a short distance from Hawick, Branxholm Castle is much altered since that mid-November night sometime in the middle of the sixteenth century when the kenspeckle Jamie Telfer of Dodhead rode up to the gate seeking assistance. Today you may stay in Branxholm Castle as it is run as a bed and breakfast establishment by the present tenants; it is however still Buccleuch property. It is the west tower which is the oldest part of Branxholm Castle today. This dates from after 1570 as in this year the Earl of Surrey carried out extensive gunpowder aided alterations. In other words he blew the place to smithereens.

There are modern additions to Branxholm but the remains of old works can be seen around the building.

But this is a far cry from poor Jamie Telfer knocking at the yett in search of succour from the bauld (bold) Buccleuch, following the theft by an English raiding party of his few cattle and insight goods — at least according to Sir Walter Scott's version. Others tell a different tale with Buccleuch in fact being the one who turned the unfortunate Jamie Telfer away. No one is certain where the Dodhead in the ballad was located; some scholars state that it lay between Teviot and Ettrick, others that it was between Teviot and Liddle.

A Dod, Dodburn and Dod Rig lie south-west of Hawick and would fit in best with the ballad's narrative. Dodhead, however, can be found north-west of Hawick on the watershed between Teviotdale and Ettrick but its geographic situation does not match the unfolding of the tale. Gibby Elliot of Stobs Ha', south of Hawick, had sent Jamie away to seek succour from those to whom he had payed blackmail at Branxholm Ha' which lies west of Hawick. Eventually on a borrowed horse along with William's Wat from Catslockhill and his two sons, Jamie arrives at Branxholm:

> And whan they come tae Branksome Ha',
> They shouted a' baith loud and hie,
> Till up and spak the bauld Buccleuch,
> Said — 'Whae's this brings the fray to me?'

Jamie explains that he has left the Fair Dodhead empty barring for a wailing wife and three children, which whether in pity for poor Jamie or the fact that he must honour the blackmail paid to him, Buccleuch sends word far and wide to gather to his cause, or else:

> Gar warn the water, braid and wide,
> Gar warn it soon and hastily!
> They that winna ride for Telfer's kye,
> Let them never look in the face o' me

> Warn Wat o' Harden and his sons,
> Wi them will Borthwick Water ride,
> Warn Gaudilands, and Allanhaugh,
> And Gillmanscleugh, and Commonside.

> Ride by the gate at Preisthaughswire,
> And warn the Currors o' the Lee,
> As ye come down the Hermitage Slack,
> Warn doughty Willie o' Gorrinberry.

Once a band has been gathered the Scots, led by Scott, set off in pursuit of the raiders who are overtaken in a running battle which sees victory for the Teviotdale men at Kershope Ford on Liddle:

> O mony a horse ran masterless,
> The splintered lances flew on hie;
> But or they won tae the Kershope ford,
> The Scots had gotten victory.

Thirty of the Captain's men lie bleeding on the ground while he himself is so wounded that his chances of future fatherhood are impossible, although Scott's version of the ballad is most delicate in the description of the injury. Adding insult to awful injury the Scots, led by a wild gallant, 'Watty wi the Wadspurs', raid the Captain's byre and removed his thirty or so cattle:

> When they come to the Fiar Dodhead,
> Thet were a welcome sight to see!
> For instead of his ain ten milk-kye,
> Jamie Telfer has got thirty and three.

> And he has paid the rescue shot,
> Baith wi' goud, and the white monie;
> And at the burial of Willie Scott,
> I wot was mony a weeping e'e.

So already knowing the ballad of Jamie Telfer and the part played by the Bauld Buccleuch, Sir Walter Scott sets the scene for the tale told by the last minstrel in his 'Lay' at Branxholm, where the cosy after dinner scene pictures knights and pages lingering around the fire, while the weary stag hounds dream of past and future hunts on the rush-clad floor. A list of the outdoors staff goes thus in the third verse of the first canto of the *Lay of the Last Minstrel*:

Nine-and-twenty knights of fame
Hung their shields in Branxholm Hall;
Nine-and-twenty squires of name
Brought them their steeds from bower to stall;
Nine-and-twenty yeomen tall,
Waited, duteous, on them all;
They were all knights of mettle true,
Kinsman of the bold Buccleuch.

Ten of them were sheathed in steel,
With belted sword and spur on heel;
They quitted not their harness bright,
Neither by day nor yet by night;
They lay down to rest
With corslet laced,
Pillowed on buckler cold and hard;
They carved at the meal with gloves of steel,
And they drank the red wine through the helmet bared.

Ten squires, ten yeomen, mail-clad men,
Waited the beck of the warders ten:
Thirty steeds both fleet and wight,
Stood saddled in stable day and night,
Barbed with frontlet of steel, I trow,
And with Jed-wood axe at saddle-bow:
A hundred more fed free in stall:-
Such was the custom of Branxholm Hall.

In other words the Scotts of Branxholm Hall were, according to the minstrel's lay, always ready for a battle with a party of thirty armed men ready to ride out at a moment's notice. Whether such was ever the custom other than in fiction is difficult to ascertain; certainly Teviotdale was right in the path of invaders from the south making some state of readiness essential at all times.

The bauld Buccleuch features in another saga of derring do, at the time when, as Scottish Warden of the West March, he was instrumental in the famous rescue of Kinmont Willie from Carlisle Castle. Willie, a descendant of the even more famous Johnnie Armstrong, more of whom shortly, had been captured by the English and flung into prison on what should have been a day of truce. This, the Scots in general and Scotts in particular, found most displeasing.

The ballad has a similar ring to *Jock o' the Side*, but instead of three going to the rescue there rides instead:

> He has call'd him forty marchmen bauld,
> Were kinsmen to the bauld Buccleuch;
> Wi'spur on heel, and splent on spauld,
> And gloves o'green, and feather blue.

Disguised as hunters, soldiers and masons, the latter group trick an enquiring English patrol that their long ladder is to assist in herrying a corbie's nest; Carlisle castle. No blood is to be spilt during the rescue, the Scottish King already has his mind set upon plonking his breeches on the Stone of Scone at Westminster. Anyway across the flooded Eden the party rides, climbs the castle wall, hacks a way through the lead roof and prison bars and rescues Kinmont Willie. Pursuit is inevitable, but while the Scots ford the flooded Eden, the Carlisle garrison can only shake their fists from the other side.

What the event did was set the March in a steerie, raids from either side becoming commonplace. Eventually a meeting of Commissioners was held at Berwick at which it was decided that Buccleuch should go in person to Queen Elizabeth and apologise. Bess took to the Borderer; in fact she wished an army of men like him for herself and the bauld Buccleuch was soon allowed to return to Branxholm.

Such was the Scotts' liking for the racy life of the Border that Branxholm was originally obtained in an exchange deal from Sir John Inglis, who found the Teviotdale life too boisterous. The then Scott property, in the relative peace of Lanarkshire at Murdieston, appealed more to John Inglis. William Scott of Buccleuch, on the other hand, was scarcely settled in when he discovered that the cattle of Cumbria were quite the equal to his own. Perhaps like stolen apples they tasted the sweeter for the method used to obtain them.

Even without twenty-nine knights and their attendant squires and yeomen, Johnnie Armstrong no doubt thought himself well prepared with his own kinsmen at his back when he set out to meet King James V at Carlenrig in July of 1530. Somewhere along the line the Border bush telegraph failed to inform Johnnie Armstrong, of Gilknockie Tower near Langholm, that the royal party did not hunt the hind or stag, but sought instead the likes of himself and his pals for a demonstration of royal justice.

Well, the occasional deer might have been chased but the historian, Lindesay of Pitscottie, relates:

After this hunting he hanged John Armstrong, Laird of Gilnockie, and his complices to the number of thirty-six persons. For which many Scottishmen heavily lamented, for he was the most redoubtable chieftain there had been, for a long time on the Borders of Scotland or England. He rode ever with twenty-four able gentlemen well horsed; yet he never molested any Scottishman. But it is said that, from the Borders to Newcastle, every man of estate paid him tribute to be free of his trouble. He came before the King with his foresaid number richly apparelled, trusting that in the free offer of his person, he should obtain the King's favour. But the King, seeing him and his men so gorgeous in apparel, with so many brave men under a tyrant's commandment, forwardly turning him about, he bade take the tyrant out of his sight, saying, 'What wants that knave that a king should have?' But John Armstrong made great offers to the King. That he would sustain himself, with forty gentlemen, ever ready at his service, on their own cost, without wronging any Scottishman; secondly, that there was not a subject in England, duke, earl, or baron, but, within a certain day, he should bring them to his Majesty, either quick or dead. At length he, seeing no hope of favour, said, very proudly: 'It is folly to seek grace at a graceless face. But, had I known this, I would have lived in the Borders despite of King Harry and you both; for I know King Harry would weigh my best horse with gold to know I was condemned to die this day.

The ballad of Johnnie Armstrong more or less follows Lindesay's narrative in his promises and final regret that he had given himself so easily when just as simply he could have evaded any force bent upon his capture.

'Had I my horse, and harness good,
And riding as I wont to be,
It would have been tauld this hundred year,
The meeting of my King and me!'

'Farewell my bonny Gilnock-ha',
Where on the Esk thou standest stout,
Gif I had lived but seven years mair,
I would have gilt thee round about.'

Johnnie murdered was at Carlinrigg,
And all his gallant companie;
But Scotland's heart was ne'er sae wae,
Tae see sae mony brave men die,

Because they saved their countrie dear,
Frae Englishmen: nane were sae bauld;
While Johnnie lived on the Border-side,
None of them durst come near his hauld.

A stone built into the dyke of Teviothead old kirkyard re-
members the passing of John Armstrong and his band, with the
quotation of the penultimate verse above. This is a modern
monument erected in 1897 when J. Kennedy, a bookseller in
Hawick, set up a subscription fund to mark the place where
Johnny and his men were murdered. It is elsewhere that the
bodies of Gilnockie and his men lie, outwith the kirkyard
marked by a sandstone stump in a fenced off section of a field
between the kirkyard and Frostlie Burn. Now owned by the Clan

Johnny Armstrong memorial at Teviothead Churchyard.

Armstrong Trust who have also provided an information board, the stump defied the efforts of a farmer and powerful tractor to move the relic.

A theory held by some of the Armstrong Trust is that what is seen today is the mere upper part of a monument, similar in height to the Milholm Cross in Liddesdale. As the Carlenrig stone lies on a flood plain it is possible that the soil level has built up over the past four hundred years and many feet below the upright may well sit in a stone base — a possible explanation as to why a hundred horsepower failed to uproot what was placed there by human toil.

Saint or sinner, patriot or traitor like many other heroes of the ballads, the true character of the real Johnnie Armstrong other than that he was held in some esteem by the people of the Borders remains uncertain. According to the ballad, clad in Sunday best, he was actually on his way to greet the king on his journey over from Ettrick, totally unsuspecting of any ill-will which James V may have felt for him.

The entry about his execution in official records is curt:- 'John Armestrange, "alias Blak Jok" and Thomas his brother convicted of common theft, and reset of theft etc — Hanged.'

Alongside the Armstrong monument in Teviothead burial ground is the one time minister of the church, Thomas Scott Riddell, author of *Scotland Yet*. The monument beyond the church is a monument to Scott Riddell raised in 1874.

At Henderson's Knowe a short distance downstream from Teviothead, the Museum of Border Arms and Armour at the Johnnie Armstrong Gallery is worth a visit by those who wish to see how the Borderers went forth to battle. Run by the Moffat family, Brian, his wife Maureen and son Kenneth, the museum has some of the earliest Scottish swords known to be in existence. Brian Moffat is no mere curator in the ordinary sense describing the exhibits from a prearranged text, but as the display is in fact the family collection he knows the history and manufacture of practically every item.

Brian Moffat travels extensively in his search for the weapons used in the many years of conflict in the Borders. From his research into arms and armour one thing is apparent, that very few edged weapons were made locally. Even in Scotland as a whole, there appears to have been a trend to import sword blades for final assembly. Some of the older weapons such as spear heads are remarkably complex in their construction, having either a soft iron core, sheathed in harder metal, or being made from laminations of steel and iron, heated almost to whiteness in the forge to be welded into a solid mass. Where body armour was concerned the Borderers, as light horsemen, did not ride forth encased in steel. Instead they wore a jack, a leather jerkin with overlapping steel plates, enough to turn a blow from an edged weapon, or a simple steel breast plate, and of course the steel bonnet, the emblem of the reiver.

Two more than life-size wooden knights guard the entrance to the Johnnie Armstrong Gallery. The work of Kenneth Moffat these make the gallery impossible to miss. As an independent museum Hendersons Knowe does not feature in official tourist guides but is one of the best displays visited in *Discovering the Borders 2*.

Around Hawick the hills are crisscrossed by a maze of B and unclassified motor roads offering ample choice for the exploring motorist. One such expedition is possible into the depths of Craik Forest which reaches from the head of Teviot across the valley of the Borthwick Water and Tilmar Water right into Ettrick. Within Craik Forest runs the line of a Roman Road, a ditto Signal Station and a million trees. Craik itself lies at the end of six miles of single track road where the Forestry Commission have provided car parking, a picnic site and a reasonable forest walk leading to a waterfall, modest in dry weather, exciting in the wet.

By taking a diversion from the B711 road leading from Teviot into Ettrick, you pass Harden House, a private residence, still the home of descendants of Auld Wat o Harden, who somehow manages to keep cropping up in other chapters of this book. The deep glen where Harden hid his stolen herds can still be seen, although the house — the private residence of Lord Polworth — is screened by trees only glimpsed from the road.

Returning to the B711 this shortly crosses the reservoir of Alemoor Loch, where the Ale Water is born by a combination of bridge and causeway. By the steep Buck Cleugh the road drops to Buccleuch where the Scott dynasty originated. Buccleuch consists of only an hotel and a few houses but an ancient church and burial ground lie nearby. Above at

Phenzhopehaugh, the name and a Motte suggest an early Norman settlement. The story of Ettrick, however, lies in another chapter.

# CHAPTER 3

## *Liddesdale*

From Teviotdale and Hawick the winding B6399 follows the Slitrig Water over the watershed into the upper part of Liddesdale, still part of Roxburgh District but one of the farthest flung outposts of the Borders Region. Newcastlton, the principal settlement in Liddesdale, for instance, is twenty miles from Hawick. Unlike other major rivers in the Borders, the Liddel does not form part of the mighty Tweed drainage system, but instead flows westwards to join the Border Esk near Canonbie before discharging into the Solway Firth. Esk and Liddel do share one common trait with the Tweed, running for the main part of their course through Scotland but discharging into the sea in England, in this instance at Sark on Sands, west of Carlisle.

River systems in their own right, Esk and Liddel have runs of salmon, but it is for the quality of the seatrout fishing that both rivers are most noted. Fortunately seatrout fishing does not enjoy the same glamour status as the pursuit of salmon. Angling permits are therefore readily available at a reasonable price for much of the Liddel, where the fishing is controlled by the Esk and Liddel Fisheries Association.

Seatrout are one of the most sporting of game fish met with on Border rivers, entering the rivers from late spring through to autumn. A 'wet' summer with plenty of water to carry the fish upstream is the wish of most seatrout anglers especially those fishing upriver beats, although some determined fish will run through from the tide with their backs virtually bare, i.e., clear of the water. A bonny fetcher is the seatrout, frequently airborne, never counted as in the bag until on the bank, especially as is the case on Liddel where attempts at its capture usually take place during the hours of darkness.

Once the twisting valley of the Slitrig provided a natural line for the Waverley route as it climbed from Teviotdale bound for Newcastleton and Carlisle. Even lacking the sea lochs and mountains of some lines in the west Highlands, the Waverley was without doubt scenic, furthermore a sair pech for the steam locomotives as they hauled their passenger or mixed goods trains from valley to valley. As was the case with the other Border railways Dr Beeching spelt the doom of the Waverley when its closure was announced in the 1960s. Protest was futile, even that of the Newcastleton minister who attempted to physically impede the progress of the last train until he was forcibly removed by the strong arm of the law.

Stobs Castle was a one-time military and p.o.w. camp making Stobs Halt one of the busiest stations in the Borders during this century's world wars. Few relics of the railway line remain. The most impressive, which can be seen from the adjacent road, is the Shankend Viaduct which spans the Langside Burn before it joins the Slitrig. Ever climbing alongside the Slitrig, Whiterope was a notoriously heavy pull for the panting steam engines which served this line before it arrived at Riccarton Junction. Riccarton, it is said, was unique, purely a railway settlement with the iron road the only access to the Junction where the Border Counties line from Hexham joined the Waverley route.

Riccarton Junction now lies deep in forestry plantations. Some idea of the importance of Riccarton which once boasted engine sheds, two signal boxes and naturally a station, can be gauged by the 50ft deep piles of engine ash which have been exploited for unburnt coal and the manufacture of building blocks.

Beyond Shankend, looking south-west from the road across the tree clad hills, the unplanted twin cones of Maiden Paps make a distinct landmark, standing stark against the dark green conifers. Around these two hills, whose shape indicates the source of their name, runs the Catrail, an ancient ditch and dyke whose origins and purpose has caused much debate among historians and continues to do so. What appears to be a firebreak through the plantations is in fact the Catrail while its line peters out against the modern road at Flosh Burn two miles farther south.

Some sources say the Catrail marked the line of Anglo-Saxon penetration westwards, a boundary between them and the Celtic people whom the invaders had expelled from the lower valleys into the uplands. Said to begin at a Torwoodlee fort and broch near Galashiels, its explanation as a boundary is certainly much more feasible than as a defensive work. From Torwoodlee the Catrail is reputed to run west for seven miles before swinging south through the valleys of Yarrow, Ettrick, Borthwick and Teviot to peter out on or near the Border having run a total of around fifty miles. Another theory considers the Catrail to be a line of communication linking the hill forts and settlements of the Romanised Britons.

Whatever its purpose, in later years the Catrail was of no consequence in the Anglo-Scottish conflict across the Cheviot range in the sixteenth century. If Teviotdale could be cited as the front line of these wars, Liddesdale was surely the forward observation post, an opinion shared by James Hogg, the Ettrick Shepherd:

> Lock the door Lauriston,
> Lion of Liddesdale,
> Lock the door Lauriston,
> Hold them at bay.
>
> Come all Northumberland,
> Teesdale and Cumberland,
> Elliot o' Lauriston,
> Elliot for ay.

Snugged right up against the Northumberland-Cumberland Border the valley of the Liddel was a law unto itself at times. This even extended to Scottish kings telling their English counterparts that they could do what they willed with the inhabitants without fear of interference from the Scottish monarchy. A meeting of Border commissioners representing both Scots and English agreed that where Liddesdale was concerned the king of England was granted 'power to invade the said inhabitants of Liddesdale, to their slaughter, burning, herships, robbing, reifing, despoiling and destruction, and so to continue the same at his Graces pleasure, till the attempts of the inhabitants were fully attoned for.'

Hard times for the folk of Liddesdale indeed; declared to be outside the law there was neither place nor person to which they could turn, other than their own kin and allies. Loyalties here were to the family clan first, then to their valley. Consideration of crown and nation came far behind the first essential

— to survive and put meat on the table. Here then, in what today is a quiet peaceful valley, there dwelt in medieval times some of the most lawless families in Britain. But it had not always been so. The Armstrongs, one of the families frequently cited as ringleaders, had previously been respected as loyal and influential. Traditionally the Armstrongs sprung from the last Anglo-Danish Earl of Northumberland, Siward Digre or Sword Strong Arm. The first time the name is recorded is however in Cumbria, where they were verderers or forest officers. It was at the Battle of the Standard that the family first obtained the English version of the name, where a Siward Digre used his Strong Arm to remount the Scottish King. Eventually the Armstrongs appeared in the Liddel and nearby valleys of the West March where the family were so numerous that they could muster a horse force of 3,000.

A change in climate and a succession of poor harvests may be the reason why during the sixteenth century robbery and rustling were at their height. Little is written of the ordinary lives led by the people of Liddesdale, or of times when the extraordinary people of Liddesdale were doing ordinary things. Really nothing has changed; the humble plodder today may toil at life's task for decades. Then one night the humble plodder gets drunk and challenges the constabulary to fight! A night in the cells and instant notoriety, or fame.

Even before the rise of the sixteenth-century reivers, Liddesdale was of considerable strategic importance as an invasion route up through the Tynedale. Not surprisingly such a valley needed something special in the way of a fortress, which it certainly has in the shape of Hermitage Castle. Hermitage never fails to surprise standing alone and aloof amid moor and moss on one of the bleakest parts of Hermitage Water. A mile up or downstream the terrain has a milder tree clad appearance, but it must be remembered that Hermitage was not built for amenity or pleasant living conditions.

A castle existed on this site, or nearby, in the mid-thirteenth century. The building was repaired by Edward I during the Scottish Wars of Independence. It was the De Soulis family, who had arrived in Scotland with David I, who are the first recorded owners of Hermitage, Lords of Liddesdale and builders of the original pile, now vanished. Like the old tower the family also

Hermitage Castle in Liddlesdale, certainly the largest ruined fortification in the Borders, Grim tales and legends surround this isolated pile.

vanished from the Border's scene in the reign of Robert the Bruce; the demise of the last of the line, Lord William, shall be dealt with shortly.

What remains of Hermitage Castle as we see it today is based upon a building begun not by the Scots, but by the English family of Dacre, sometime in the mid-fourteenth century. The central core of the castle, which forms the oldest part of the building, is cited as being typical of an English fortified manor house of this period.

Extensions by the Douglas family brought Hermitage into line with other Scottish tower houses — the three smaller rectangular towers being added prior to 1400 and the larger tower on the south-west corner a little later. Minor additions and alterations continued through to the sixteenth century, while the corbelled parapet and crowstepped gables of the eastern towers are nineteenth-century additions made when extensive repairs were undertaken to Hermitage's tumbling walls by the duke of Buccleugh. Since 1930 Hermitage Castle and the nearby chapel have been in the care of the state, now under the stewardship of 'Historic Scotland', who maintain this and other notable buildings including the Border abbeys. Hermitage Castle is the major and only remaining keep in the valley of the Liddel. Of the towers belonging to the Armstrongs and their allies next to nothing remains; all places of strength were flung down on the orders of James VI, following his ascension to the united kingdom. Some of these, according to accounts, were crude in the extreme. The duchess of Cumberland — or was it Northumberland — compared the home of the celebrated raider Jock o' the Side with the humblest dog kennel in England. This was a trifle ungrateful considering she had sheltered there when fleeing, following her husband's failed uprising against the English crown — even if the Liddesdale men did steal her horses.

An early religious chapel which seems to have been attached to Kelso Abbey, gave both Hermitage Castle and the burn it stands beside their names but did nothing to inspire any saintly acts by later inhabitants. Hermitage Castle was the home of the de Soulis family, who had served the Kings of Scots with distinction and had been Scottish ambassadors to the French court. Sir John de Soulis, who fell at the battle of Dundalk in Ireland, was, with John Comym, a Guardian of Scotland from 1298 until his death.

It was Lord William who was destined to be the last of the clan, due perhaps to his own ambition to be king. But tradition records that Lord Soulis had acquired a reputation for being a dabbler in the black arts, which, combined with a fearsome physical strength, held the countryside in fear and terror of his actions. Complaint after complaint was put to the king, who seemed reluctant to act personally with regard to Soulis's behaviour which allegedly included continued plotting to usurp Bruce. Eventually exasperated, the Bruce's answer to yet another party of petitioners was 'Boil him if you please'.

This was duly done by wrapping Soulis in a sheet of lead in a cauldron on Nine Stane Rig near Hermitage; but not before a struggle, as Lord Soulis had the assistance of Redcap, a spirit said to haunt the castle, whose last instruction was for the key to be thrown over the unfortunate lord's left shoulder on leaving the gates for the last time.

Scott's *Minstrelsy* contains a work by Dr John Leyden on the demise of Lord Soulis which involves Thomas of Ersyltoun, armed with Michael Scott's book of spells and the rescue of the heir of Branxholm. Since ropes or chains will not hold Soulis whether on account of his strength or magic, the lead sheet is the last fatal resort.

> They rol'd him up in a sheet of lead,
> A sheet of lead for a funeral pall;
> They plunged him in the cauldron red,
> and melted him, lead, bones and all.

> At the Skelf-hill, the cauldron still
> The men of Liddesdale can shew;
> And on the spot, where they boiled the pot,
> The spreat and the deer hair ne'er shall grow.

History, however, records that Lord Soulis did not meet this grisly end but died a prisoner within the walls of Dumbarton Castle, where he had been incarcerated following his capture at Berwick-on-Tweed.

Another work by Leyden the 'Cout of Keeldar', also in the *Minstrelsy*, tells of the murder of this young Northumberland chief who sallied across the Border to hunt in Liddesdale, despite the threatening presence of Lord Soulis at Hermitage. From the very first line the 'Cout of Keeldar' begs to be read.

> The eiry blood-hound howled by night,
> The streamers flaunted red,
> Till broken streaks of flaky light,
> O'er Keelders mountains spread.

Such was his physique that this laird, from what we now know as Kielder in Northumberland, was called the cout or colt. Before setting off to hunt in Liddesdale his wife warns him not to go; yet confident in his own prowess, with lucky charms of holly and rowan in his plume, young Keeldar feels that he is more than a match for even Soulis's invincible axe, formed of earth-fast flint.

After encountering a strange little man who emerges from below the heath and riding around the Kielder Stone the Cout and his hunting party arrive at Hermitage. An invitation to dine is accepted, the Cout warning his men to be on their guard and ready to fight should the 'bull's head', a signal for assassination, appear on the table. As the feast nears its end the bull's head is set on the board; unfortunately the Cout's men are all frozen, enchanted, into inaction — all except the chief who, with his magic charms, is immune not only from the enchantment suffered by his men but also from physical harm. No spear, sword or arrow can pierce his armour until the fray reaches Hermitage Water where Keeldar's lucky charms are broken by the flowing stream and he is defenceless as his attackers drive him into a deep pool to be drowned.

> The holly floated to the side,
> And the leaf of the rowan pale:
> Alas! no spell could charm the tide,
> Nor the lance of Liddesdale.

> Swift was the Cout o' Keeldar's course,
> Along the lily lee;
> But home came never hound nor horse,
> And never home came he.

The 'Cout of Keeldar' is a 'modern' ballad from the nineteenth century, based on the fate of the young Chief of Mangerton who was lured to Hermitage and murdered at a feast. One story of the event relates that Lord Soulis had been caught in the act of abducting a young girl and somehow Mangerton had saved him from the punishment he deserved, but in the lingo of the present-day gangster movie 'knew to much for his own good'. A grass-covered mound eleven feet long, outwith the old chapel graveyard, is said to be the grave of the Cout of Keeldar. Beside the B6357 a mile south of Newcastleton, the Millholm Cross marks the spot where young Armstrong of Mangerton's followers rested before they bore his body to the burial ground of Edelston on the slopes of Kirk Hill above.

Hermitage, it seems, brings out the worst in men in legend and fact, as was the case of Sir William Douglas, 'the dark knight of Liddesdale' known also as the 'Flower of Chivalry'. It was he who tarnished that title and the Douglas name by his fiendish treatment of Sir Alexander Ramsay of Dalhousie, his replacement in the post of Sheriff of Roxburgh. Sir William Douglas had been one of the chief defenders of Scotland following the Scottish defeat at Halidon Hill near Berwick-on-Tweed in 1333. In the years which followed this Scottish defeat, Balliol, who had been declared king by Edward III, more or less handed over all the south of Scotland into English control.

At this time David II, son and heir to Robert the Bruce, was only about nine years old, and fled into exile for nine years. So persistent were the efforts of Sir William and others in harrying the north-east of England that by 1341 it was possible for David II to return to Scotland. Meantime Balliol had fled the country while Edward III had embarked on a war with the French which was to last a hundred years, and for a period English attentions to the south of Scotland fell into decline.

Why William Douglas, after a lifetime of patriotic service, had Ramsay seized while presiding over a court at Hawick's St Mary's in 1342, is not known. Whatever the reason the unfortunate man was carried off to Hermitage, where he was thrown into a dungeon to starve to death.

Among the many legends and half-truths surrounding Hermitage Castle that of Ramsay is authentic; the other familiar true story concerns Mary Queen of Scots and James Hepburn, Earl of Bothwell. Were Bothwell alive today he perhaps would have been known as 'a bit of a lad'. In 1566 he was suspected of being more than just a good friend to Queen Mary.

One of the most powerful barons in Scotland, Bothwell was at the time Keeper of Liddesdale, holder of Hermitage and Lieutenant of the Marches in Scotland. This was a peculiar time for Reformation Scotland with a young Catholic queen, who, already widowed, had returned from France five years previously to be Queen of Scots. By 1565 she was married again to Lord Darnley whom she had only known for a few weeks, although an early infatuation seems to have quickly cooled. Already, in March 1566 when Mary was six months pregnant, her Italian secretary David Riccio had been murdered after being dragged from her side in Holyrood Palace. Darnley had led the execution squad to the Queen's supper chamber by a private stair, little knowing that he himself would face assassination the following year.

Therefore in late 1566 Mary was still married to Darnley but had developed an admiration for Bothwell, who despite any other failings had remained loyal. Perhaps hoping to impress the queen further, Bothwell set out to put the clans of Liddesdale in order prior to Mary's judicial visit to Jedburgh.

This was easier said than done, even with an initial success of taking several Elliots prisoner into Hermitage, before setting out for further prey. Among those he proposed casting into dungeons — akin today to fresh coats of paint on everything prior to a royal visit — was one Little Jock Elliot of the Park. Eventually Bothwell caught up with Little Jock who was shot from his horse. With confidence Bothwell approached the fallen man to 'mak siccar' as to the reiver's state of health or otherwise, whereupon Little Jock leapt up and proceeded to inflict multiple stab wounds upon the Earl with a sharp instrument before expiring himself.

Or did he die? Accounts of Little Jock's demise may have been exaggerated, as seventeen years later in the Border Papers the people of Redesdale are complaining about the thieving activities of the Liddesdale men including one 'John Elvat of the Park'. Where and when Little Jock met his end must remain a mystery but the verse from his ballad is said to date from the year following the affray with Bothwell and sounds much more like a boast than a lament for a dead reiver.

'I've vanquished the Queen's Lieutenant,
And garr'd her troopers flee,
My name is Little Jock Elliot
And wha dar meddle wi me.'

It can be assumed that the Earl of Bothwell would be bleeding profusely from Little Jock's farewell, as he suffered the indignity of being hauled home on the back of a cart. Here, adding insult to injury, it was found that the captive Elliots now held Hermitage and would only allow the Earl entry on the promise of freedom from persecution. It was to visit Bothwell on his sick bed that Queen Mary made the famous ride from Jedburgh to Hermitage, and in doing so catching a fever from which she all but died.

The Little Jock affair must have rankled Bothwell as in 1567 the following year he was trying to mount a raid into Liddesdale against the Elliots and their ilk. However, by now Mary's second husband Lord Darnley was dead in rather suspicious circumstances, suspected as a collaborator in Darnley's death and Bothwell, now married to the Queen, was decidedly not flavour of the month among the Border chieftains. The popularity of both the Queen and Bothwell was on a decided downturn; no leader was going to risk an association in such circumstances, leaving the Earl's humiliation by Little Jock unrevenged, if the Borderer did in fact survive their earlier encounter.

If Yarrow is the home of the romantic ballad, Liddesdale is that of the historic. Right slap bang on the English Border where the counties of Northumberland and Cumberland meet, there is little wonder that the bards of old found plenty of material here. Across dale and fell they rode into the pages of history, ballad and legend: the Elliots and Armstrongs, Lindsays and Grahams, a race of men whose Christian names and surnames were shared by so many others in the same valley that they were commonly known by their nicknames or the place names of their towers clustered around the Liddel. Jock o' the Side, Hughie the Graeme, Kinmont Willie, Hobbie Noble — an Englishman banished over the Border — were men who in ballad form at least rode to Newcastle or Carlisle to free from prison their captured fellows.

Jock o' the Side was an Armstrong, perhaps a nephew of the clan chief the laird of Mangerton; his notoriety is mentioned in a quotation in Chapter 1 of this book. In Scott's *Minstrelsy* he merits a complete ballad, a story of his capture and rescue from prison and the hangman's rope in Newcastle.

> Now Liddesdale has ridden a raid,
> But I wat they had better staid at hame;
> For Michael o' Winfield he is dead,
> And Jock o' the Side is prisoner ta'en.

His mother pleads with her brother, Mangerton, to send a party to effect a rescue. The clan chief declines but delegates three of his best, his sons, the Laird's Jock, the Laird's Wat plus Hobbie Noble. At Newcastle the three rescuers find the gates locked against them, the notched pole they have brought too short to scale the walls. This is however no deterrent for the bold trio; the gate porter has his neck wrung, his keys taken and Jock o the Side is released from prison complete with:

Full fifteen stane o' Spanish iron,
They hae laid a' right sair on me;
Wi' locks and keys I am fast bound
Into this dungeon dark and dreirie.

Still bound in chains the Laird's Jock hoists the prisoner on his back and soon they are fleeing homewards, the chains forcing Jock o the Side to ride sidesaddle.

Jock! sae winsomely's ye ride,
Wi' baith your feet upon ae side;
Sae weel y'er harniest and sae trig,
I troth ye sit like ony bride.

At Cholerford an auld man tells them that never in his lifetime has he seen the Tyne run so high in flood. Alas there is a troop of twenty horse in pursuit from Newcastle and now the Liddesdale men are between these sharp pointed weapons and the deep fast-flowing Tyne. But cross they do, leaving the land-sergeant on the south bank pleading for at least the return of the fetters. No chance; the Laird's Jock mockingly tells him that the chains will make fine shoes for his gude bay mare who has carried him safely across the flood.

So it can be seen that not only were the Liddesdale men constantly goading the English but also that in their activities they raised the ire of Scottish Kings. Johnnie Armstrong was perhaps unfortunate because, in many instances when reprisals were planned against Liddesdale, the inhabitants simply vanished west into Tarras Moss or the hidden fastness of the Border Hills; or hearing that a punitive force was riding their way might in turn raid that force's keep or castle. This ploy was used by the above Johnnie Armstrong in 1528 when, forewarned of Lord Darce's intention, he was busy about Darce's tower at Netherby in Cumberland while Darce was firing Gilnockie.

While in feudal times the main focus of attention was upon Hermitage, the modern capital of Liddesdale is the town of Newcastleton which celebrated its bicentenary in 1993. Of course in Border terms that makes Newcastleton a fairly modern place, the town being a planned settlement established with the aid of the duke of Buccleuch in 1793.

Around this time the valleys around Liddesdale were

suffering from depopulation; sheep runs were replacing arable farming and many small landholders were facing eviction. This trend began following the Union of the Crowns when a selection of Armstrongs, Elliots, Grahams and other riding families of the western middle march had been forcefully deported to Europe and Ireland from whence they emigrated to the Colonies.

The Armstrongs in particular seem to have suffered more than others as there are few families of that name left in Liddesdale today. Somehow the Grahams have managed to stage a comeback despite what was virtual banishment in the early seventeenth century and the name is still relatively common in the Borders and Liddesdale.

Whether they were forced to leave or departed voluntarily is debatable, but the Clan Armstrong Trust can trace the clan's progress down the valley of the North Tyne with a brief sojourn at Haltwhistle. Eventually many Armstrongs settled in and around Tyneside, where here today they number in the thousands and Armstrongs claim that there are more of them around Newcastle than there are Smiths.

Established as a weaving village the town is never referred to as Newcastleton by its people. The old name Copshawholm, after the level piece of land where the town was established, or simply the Holm, is always used in preference. The Holm is unique among Border towns; first it is a planned settlement,

Douglas Square, Newcastleton, a pleasant corner of the Borders.

with the broad straight main street stretching into the distance, Douglas Square in the centre and two minor squares north and south making tree-shaded havens in the height of summer.

Side streets lead off at right angles forming the back rows of the Holm into precise rectangular blocks reaching down to the riverside where the Liddel washes the town's outskirts. And amazingly the streets are level, flat, sans hill sans brae — practically every other Border town struggles uphill from river valleys but no so the Holm. The sheltered flood plain of the Liddel has provided an ideal site for the newest of Border towns.

This cross is said to mark the site of Old Castleton, high on the moorland. The castle which gave the town its name occupied a site where cattle are grazing in the background.

Weaving never became properly established at Copshawholm; instead the town became quite a noted centre for shoe and clog making, the latter still carried on until recent years.

No one would deny that the Holm occupies an isolated situation. Do not imagine however that it is bleak; here the valley of the Liddle is broad and fertile. As the 'New' part of the name suggests there already was a Castleton in the Liddel Valley. This lies upstream near a burial ground. A mound of earth is the only vestige of the 'castle' while in the field opposite the stump of sandstone may have been the market cross for the settlement here, high on Castleton Muir.

From where it rises near the English border on Deadwater Fell until where it leaves the Borders Region at Kershopefoot the valley of the Liddel offers a diverse and varied landscape. Mostly the result of the hand of man, the scrubby woodland which hid the comings and goings in medieval times has vanished, first under the hooves and questing grasp of grazing sheep. Then this century vast acreages of hill and fell have been transformed into man-made forests.

Forests on the Scottish side of the Border, those of Wauchope, Newcastleton and Kershope, form part of the Border Forest Park, joined in England by Kielder Forest — the largest man-made forest in Europe which now contains, in Kielder Water, the largest artificial lake in Europe.

Forestry tracks reach out from Newcastleton itself, routes to suit the walker, or rider on mountain bike or horse, the two latter being available as organised outings from Newcastleton. The Bloody Bush Road is one of the most interesting being a one-time toll road for the carriage of coal and lime from Northumberland to Scotland.

Liddesdale, as mentioned, was the heart of the Armstrong country and here at Newcastleton in Douglas Square, The Clan Armstrong Trust has established a visitor and exhibition centre dedicated to the history of the Armstrong family in particular, and Liddesdale in general. Situated appropriately in Janet Armstrong House information displayed here suggested that the prime cause for the ascendancy of the Border reivers was a mini-ice age which occurred in the sixteenth century when the cattle-stealing trade was at its height. This, combined with overpopulation of the valleys where hunger provided the driving force, led to a century of mayhem which only really ended when James VI, King of Scots, became James I of Great Britain.

At the height of the troubled times in the sixteenth century the Armstrongs could raise 3000 horses, not that their allegiance was always to the Scottish Crown as some of the clan fought for the English at the Battle of Solway Moss. There was nothing unusual in this as it appears to have been a regular occurrence with many famous Border families; like others they suffered following the Union of the Crowns and were deported en masse. On the other hand the Scotts of Buccleuch gained land; a knack of being on the right side led to the Scotts gaining parts of the Borders once the territory of the Armstrongs and Grahams.

Even so the prospect of peace in the valleys under a united crown did not appeal to all Borderers especially the Armstrong Chief, the tenth laird of Mangerton. In what came to be known as 'Ill Will Week', Mangerton led a raid deep into Cumbria in an attempt to thwart the Union of the Crowns and was captured and hung at the Grassmarket in Edinburgh. His son fled to England vanishing from the pages of history, leaving the Armstrongs to this day without a Chief of linear descent from the Mangerton branch.

Constantly members of the Trust are involved in research into the family history, currently the records are being computerised for ease of access, while field work reveals Armstrong connections far beyond the valley of the Liddel. After all an Armstrong has trod upon the moon's surface. Some idea of the dedication Clan Armstrong Trust members put into the Centre can be found in its weekend manning by Tyneside Armstrongs happy to make the 200-mile trip for an unpaid stint of duty.

Its isolation on a B road gives Newcastleton an independence and a community spirit even stronger than is found elsewhere in the Borders. Seemingly there is, 'always something on' in Newcastleton, if the number of events advertised on the notice board in Douglas Square is anything to go by. There are social and entertaining occasions all organised from within, from craft fairs to dances, not forgetting the Newcastleton Folk Festival but the main event of the year is without a doubt the Holm Show.

Established in 1893 a hundred years after the village, the full title of the event being the Liddesdale Agricultural Society's Open 'Holm Show'. The official programme gives around 335 classes and 1000 entrants for the Holm Show, so it is no small event. First in the catalogue are the fifty-five classes for sheep, which does not mean there are fifty-five breeds. No star of stage or screen can claim to receive the treatment given to the entrants in the sheep classes at the Holm Show. Nor would many of them want to appear for the prize money provided by local sponsors: £4 for first; £2 for second and £1 for third.

No, it's not the money which is prized, rather the red ticket which says 'First'. That is only to be gained after the careful selection of the beasts to be shown, a session of scrubbing and dipping on the farm before the final touch-up prior to the serious matter of judging. Rams' horns glisten with linseed oil (or is it some secret potion?); any wisps of wool are carefully trimmed and a final brush-down completes the job.

Stick dressing, floral art, baking and photography are but a few of the classes in the industrial sections. Outdoors a display of vintage tractors and vehicles adds a nostalgic touch; ponies jump in the main ring while for the energetic there is the grunt and groan of Cumberland and Westmoreland wrestling and for the super energetic a fell race. These then are but a few of the attractions of the Holm Show, a pleasant way to spend the last Saturday in August. Monday sees a further event in the Holm sheep dog trials where handlers from the Borders and beyond compete in the double lift trial.

You'll hear at the Holm Show a mixture of accents from both sides of the Border, those of Teviot and Liddesdale mingling with Cumbria and Northumbria. Scottish-English feuds have been laid to rest centuries ago. But what about the decision of the late Nicholas Ridley to select, upon being granted a life peerage, the title Baron of Liddesdale, or, as it is officially gazetted, 'Baron Ridley of Liddesdale, of Willimontswick in Northumberland'.

Baron Ridley's choice of title was not popular in Liddesdale. Correspondence in *The Scotsman* upon the subject included a letter from Lady Frances Eliott, now deceased, of Redheugh in Liddesdale, in which she likens this to a modern form of reiving. 'He that filches from me my good name robs me of that which not enriches him, and makes me poor indeed.'

A number of roads are open to the motorist on leaving Copshawholm. Here is a suggestion. Take the minor road on the west side of Douglas Square in the town, passing a monument to John Dyers, Bard of Liddesdale who died in 1968.

Where-er on earth I wander
Till life's spark does fail
I'll mind the grand historic spots
In auld Liddel's bonny vale.

The nine miles across to the Langholm–Hawick A7 road take in as wild a part of the Borders as the motorist is likely to encounter; in fact straight through the waste land of Tarras Moss where in past years the folk of Liddesdale hid from the persecution they were subjected to by the English and their own sovereigns. From where the road joins the A7 the way back to the Borders lies east, gained at the watershed at the Mosspaul Inn — the original said to have been established by the monks of Melrose as a shelter for travellers beside a chapel dedicated to St Paul. From here we must make tracks towards what is the heart of Border Ballad Country, the valleys of the Yarrow and Ettrick.

# CHAPTER 4

## Ettrick and Yarrow

Once around the valleys of Ettrick, Yarrow and Tweed the surrounding uplands were clothed in natural woodland. This, the Ettrick Forest, part of the ancient Forest of Caledon was for long a favourite hunting ground of Scottish kings right up to the Stuart dynasty. The term forest, as it was used in ancient Scotland, meant a hunting ground, rather than purely woodland, as we understand the term today, although the old meaning remains in common usage in the Scottish Highlands as deer forest. Within the Ettrick Forest would have been a mixture of Scots pine, alder, hazel, oak and birch interspaced with open areas of heather and moorgrasses. Here was a habitat providing both food and shelter to the beasts of the chase, the red and roe deer, the latter still common in the area today.

An increase in the numbers of sheep instigated by James V, brought about the eventual demise of the forest and a major alteration of the landscape. Grazing prevented the trees' natural regeneration; the hopeful seedlings seeking the spring sunlight were chopped off in their infancy by the forerunners of the blackface sheep which still dot the hillsides today. The rounded grass and heather-clad hills we see today and accept as natural are a result of changes begun five hundred years ago.

Ettrick and upper Tweed are now heavily afforested, but in Yarrow new plantations do not dominate the valley as yet. Due to their remote situation the woollen industry of Tweed and Teviot never penetrated into the valleys of Yarrow and Ettrick. Here the emphasis remains as it has always done on rural skills, sheep husbandry, the maintenance of the land in agriculture and forestry.

Yarrow (the name is a derivation of rushing water) is Ballad Country with capital letters. Because of all the valleys and dales in the Borders, nay in Scotland, that of Yarrow has more historic lore recorded in song and verse than any other. Over and above the well-known traditional ballads associated with Yarrow, writers down the ages have sung the praises of Yarrow in poem and prose. Scott, Hogg, Christopher North and Wordsworth all made their contribution; one of the earliest lines are by the poet Gavin Dunbar writing in the reign of James IV in his 'Thistle and the Rose'.

And to gar flowris compeir of all fassoun,
Full craftley conjurt scho the Yarrow,
Quilk did furth swirk als swift as any arrow.

If all the incidents related in the traditional ballads are based on fact Yarrow must have seen its fair share of murder and mayhem, elopement and deadly blood feud. At this distance in time we may never really know who composed the ballads associated with Yarrow, which in Scott's *Minstrelsy* fall into the 'Romantic' section. A theory exists perpetuated by John Leyden that many of the ballads were composed by a young man kidnapped in infancy from England by Walter Scott of Harden, at a time when he lived at Old Kirkhope behind the village of Ettrick Bridge.

Of milder mood the gentle captive grew,
Nor loved the scenes that scared his infant view;
In vales remote, from camps and castles far,
He shunned the fearful, shuddering joy of war;
Content the loves of simple swains to sing,

He, nameless as the race from hence he sprung,
Saved other names, and left his own unsung.

Happy endings are rare in the Romantic Ballad; their scribe, whoever he was, has a lot to answer for where the Yarrow Valley is concerned. 'The Dowie Dens o' Yarrow', arguably the best known of all Yarrow ballads, does not reflect the appearance of the valley. Perhaps the title, which is also a chorus line, echoes a sombre mood when cloud hangs low over Mountbenger Law or Glengaber Hill; yet in this it would differ from no other upland valley in such circumstances. No, Yarrow is no more or less than a most picturesque upland valley, wooded in the lower reaches, with the A708 road running alongside the stream when space permits or high above and distant across the broad haugh.

Around Bowhill there are fairly large plantations of conifers interspaced with larches while higher up the valley small patches of trees form shelterbelts for the streamside farms. Here and there can be caught a glimpse of what the Ettrick Forest must have looked like with odd patches of scrub oak, birch and ash, and on the wetter ground alder, as is found between the A708 and St Mary's Loch. Between Henderland and St Mary's church-yard a steep scree slope, to which sheep do not appear to have access, has a thicket of hazel bushes. Permutations of some of the above must have been features of the old Forest.

Villages cling to the roadside: Yarrowford below Hanging-shaw; Yarrow itself and Yarrowfeus with its school and a straggle of houses beside the road. Many of the hills climbing from the Yarrow Valley are predominantly grass covered al-though heather acreage is also significant. Between Bowerhope Law and Peat Law on the south side of St Mary's Loch there is now a large forestry block, but mainly this is sheep and cattle country. Grass is the main crop grown for hay or silage as winter stock feed in the improved pastures around the river, but for most of the valley the plough is a relative stranger to the ground today.

Back to the ballads however. The first to be encountered, 'Tamlane', is associated with Carterhaugh above where Yarrow and Ettrick meet.

> O I forbid ye, maidens a',
> That wear goud in your hair,
> To come and gae by Carterhaugh;
> For young Tamlane is there.

The ballad goes on with seduction on Carterhaugh amid ex-cuses of the end result on Janet the heroine.

> Out then spak her father dear,
> And he spak meik and mild —
> 'And ever alas! my sweet Janet,
> I fear ye gae with child.'

> 'And, if I be with child, father,
> Myself maun bear the blame;
> There's ne'er a knight about your ha'
> Shall hae the bairnie's name.'

Eventually she meets up with young Tamlane again who claims he has been under the spell of the Queen of Fairies since he was nine years old.

> 'The Queen of Fairies keppit me,
> In yon green hill to dwell;
> And I'm a fairy, lyth and limb;
> Fair ladye, view me well.'

Despite sorcery and trickery Janet manages to regain Tamlane on the night of Hallowe'en which is just as well as this is the time the Fairy Queen must pay her *teind* to hell, and that *tiend* could well be Tamlane. The Queen is most displeased:

> 'Had I but kenn'd Tamlane,' she says,
> 'Before ye came frae hame —
> I wad tane out your heart o' flesh,
> Put in a heart o' stane.'

Let us hope that Tamlane and the brave fair Janet who faced

Newark Tower, where passed the Minstrel in Scott's fictional work, *The Lay of the Last Minstrel*.

the elfin host after midnight on Halloween lived happily ever
after, as all good fairy tales should end. In his *The Ballads of
Scotland* William E. Aytoun cites 'Tamlane' as having appeared
in print as early as 1549 in the *Complaynt of Scotland* published
at St Andrews.

To present-day tastes the poetical works of Scott, rather than
his collected works may sound somewhat tedious and need to
be read with dedication but how about this introduction to the
'Lay of the Last Minstrel' set at Newark Castle.

> The way was long, the wind was cold,
> The Minstrel was infirm and old;
> His withered cheeks and tresses gray,
> Seemed to have known a better day;
> The harp, his one remaining joy,
> Was carried by an orphan boy;
> The last of all the Bards was he,
> Who sung of Border Chivalry.

In these lines it is easy to picture the fallen entertainment
idol as he struggles up Yarrow side.

> Old times were changed, old manners gone;
> A stranger filled the Stuart's throne;
> The bigots of an iron time
> Had called his harmless art a crime.

Tired, cold and hungry:

> He passed where Newark's stately tower
> Looks out from Yarrow's birchen bower.

The Minstrel does strike it lucky at Newark where the Lady
gives orders for the old man to be fed and offered accommodation which he repays in the recitation of 'The Lay', Scott's
first poetical work. It's a lang story based around Branxholm
Castle in Teviotdale, involving witchcraft, digging up the dead
by moonlight, mortal combat and all the ingredients which go
to make up a good tale by the Wizard.

*The Lay of the Last Minstrel* concludes with the old man settling
in his small cottage in the shadow of Newark's walls.

So passed the winter's day; but still,
When summer smiled on sweet Bowhill,
And July's eve with balmy breath,
Waved the blue-bell on Newark heath,
When throstles sang on Hare-head shaw,
And corn was green on Carterhaugh;
And flourished, broad Blackandro's oak,
The aged harper's soul awoke!


And noble youths the strain to hear,
Forsook the hunting of the deer;
And Yarrow, as he rolled along,
Bore burden to the minstrel's song.

A 'New werke' is mentioned in a charter granted to Archibald Earl of Douglas in 1423 during the reign of James I. While it was supposedly a Royal Hunting Lodge Newark remained in Douglas hands until the family fell from favour, being defeated by James II at the Battle of Arkinholm in 1455. Perhaps in 1455 it was still under construction, its date of completion being sometimes given as 1466. As the name suggests Newark is a replacement for an older nearby building Auldwark, possibly dating from the time of Alexander III, or even earlier when Ettrick was a royal forest. James IV included Newark in his dowry to Margaret Tudor, who following James's death and married to the Earl of Angus, complained that she was denied the 4000 merk rent of The Forest including Newark, and even entry to the castle by the Duke of Buccleuch.

By 1532 the tower was occupied by the Scotts of Buccleuch and major improvements took place towards the end of the seventeenth century by Anna, Duchess of Monmouth and Buccleuch. This is the lady of Scott's 'Lay of the Last Minstrelsy', Duchess of Buccleuch in her own right. Her husband, the Duke of Monmouth, an illegitimate son of King Charles II, was executed in 1685 for leading a rebellion against King James II. Anna was the last of the Buccleuchs to reside in Newark Tower; as the Border became pacified the emphasis was towards comfort rather than defence. In the early eighteenth century the Scotts of Buccleuch abandoned Newark for the comforts of a new mansion house at Bowhill, built 1708. Unlike Newark the original mansion-house at Bowhill has now disappeared, the present Borders' seat of the Buccleuch's being built in 1812, with extensions added throughout the nineteenth century.

Surrounding the name 'Scott of Buccleuch' is the legend of John Scott, who with his brother had fled from Galloway and due to their skills had been given employment by the keeper of the Forest. While the Scottish King Kenneth MacAlpin was hunting in Ettrick Forest a stag was raised which fled into terrain so steep that the mounted hunters were unable to continue the pursuit. At a place now known as Buccleugh Glen, the stag turned on the hounds where John Scott, on foot, was able to seize the animal by the antlers and carry it before the king. Most likely the deer in question was a roe buck rather than a red deer stag, as the latter would have formed more than an adequate armful for John Scott of Galloway, who from that day was to be known by royal decree as Scott of Bucks Cleugh or Buccleuch.

> . . . old Buccleuch the name did gain,
> When in the cleugh the buck was ta'en.

Certainly it makes a nice story although the name is first recorded in written documents in the early part of the eleventh century. No matter from where the line sprung the Scotts of Buccleuch and their kinsmen played a high profile role in the Border country right up to and following the Union of the Crowns. Buccleuch Scotts were Wardens of the Marches, died at Flodden alongside James IV, played a vital role at Ancrum Moor and generally kept the country on the boil for centuries.

Eventually they married into the Douglas family to inherit the title of Duke of Queensberry along with the triple barrelled surname of Montagu-Douglas-Scott. With this marriage by the 3rd Duke to Lady Montagu came the house and estate of Drumlanrig in Dumfriesshire, which shares the name of the Scott's one-time town house in Hawick, 'The Black Tower of Drumlanrig'.

Bowhill House and Country Park are open to the public during the summer season with enough features to occupy the visitor for an entire day. These may be simply a walk around the grounds which include an artificial lake where trout angling is available, horse riding or mountain bike outings.

Bowhill features one of the best adventure playgrounds for children in the Borders with ariel walkways through the tree-tops, giant slides and wild west forts. In the mid 1980s the Buccleuch Heritage Trust was formed, its aims being to make full use of Bowhill and its important collections of fine arts for educational purposes. An education officer for the house, which is open all year round by appointment for educational purposes, and a countryside ranger, are employed by the Trust. The house itself contains a number of fine paintings including Van Dycks hung in the Gallery Hall. Leaving Bowhill, a short distance up Yarrow on the north bank at Foulshiels can be found the birthplace in 1771 of African explorer Mungo Park. By 1797 aged only 26, Park had already made an expedition to Africa in search of the source of the Niger. The late eighteenth century was a remarkable time for Border talent, Park being a contemporary of Scott. Sir Walter in fact met Mungo Park flinging stones into a deep Yarrow pool, a pastime which Mungo explained to the the poet as follows. Counting the time it took for air bubbles to ascend gave some idea if a river, be it the Yarrow, or African, was fordable.

Was it mentioned earlier that more than any other the valley of Yarrow is ballad country! Well, here's another, 'The Sang of the Outlaw Murray', a battle of wills between Murray of Haningshaws and King James IV. The Murray family held the sheriffdom of Ettrick Forest from around 1450, acquiring Philiphaugh in 1461 in a grant by Lord James Douglas. Among John Murray's titles (incidentally the family name at the time was De Morvia) was Herdsman to the Queen and Keeper of Newark Castle. The Outlaw Murray of the ballad may have been the grandson of John, the first Murray of Philiphaugh, was installed as Sheriff of The Forest in 1509 but was later slain, allegedly on the instigation of Wicked Wat Scott of Buccleugh.

For a Yarrow tale 'The Outlaw Murray' does not have a grisly end with weeping widows dragging blood-stained spouses to their last resting place. Scott in his *Minstrelsy of the Scottish Border* argues the case for Hangingshaw against Newark as being the home of The Outlaw, despite the latter being the scene according to local tradition. This is highly improbable, as Newark was always a Royal Fortress.

> Ettrick Foreste is a feir foreste,
> In it grows mony a semelie trie;
> There's hart and hynd, and dae and rae,
> And of a' wild beastes grete plentie.

At Hangingshaws in what is said to have been a splendid castle, now vanished, lived the Outlaw Murray in kingly style with five hundred followers clad in Lincoln green. World reaches King James in Edinburgh who thinking that he is king of all Scotland swears that he will be king of Ettricke Foreste or the Outlaw Murray shall be King of Scotlande. An emissary is sent in the shape of James Boyd to invite the Outlaw to come to Edinburgh under safe conduct to inform King James for whom he holds the forest, remembering that James IV was not adverse to large-scale expeditions into the Borders to exert his authority over the unruly inhabitants.

Included in the invitation is a threat if the outlaw should refuse the royal request.

> 'Thou may'st vow I'll cast his castell down,
> And make a widow o' his gay ladye;
> I'll hang his merry men payr by payr,
> In ony firth where I may them see.'

James Boyd reaches Hangingshaw and is received most courteously by Murray: the royal request is, however, refused.

> 'Thir landis are *mine*!' the Outlaw said;
> 'I ken nae King in Christentie;
> Frae Soudron I this Foreste wan,
> Whan King and his knoights were not to see.'

Back in Edinburgh James Boyd gives King James the Outlaw's response much to the royal displeasure. Word is sent to the barons of Perthshire and Angus, the three Lothians and Fife to make ready for an outing to Ettrick Forest. Word of this assembly reaches Murray, who in turn enlists the help of the Border lairds from Moffatdale to Traquair. Soon King James arrives in the Borders crossing the Tweed at Caddon Ford; Hamilton, one of the party, urges James to have a council of war before embarking any further on the venture. Walter Scott of Buccleugh however urges action; whether this is because he and Murray are far from bosom pals, or whether the crafty laird has his eye on adding to his land holdings is not known. King James, as would be said today in the Borders, cuts him off by the stocking tops.

'Now had thy tongue, Sir Walter Scott,
Nor speak of reif nor felonie:
For, had everye honeste man his ain kye,
A right puir clan thy name would be.'

Anyway a meeting is arranged between the King and Outlaw Murray, each accompanied by earls of their choice to thrash out the matter in a diplomatic manner. There are threats from either side but a compromise is reached when Murray in a symbolic gesture hands the king his castle keys, whereupon he is appointed sheriffe of Ettricke Foreste along with a free pardon for him and his men.

Wha ever heard, in ony times,
Sicken an Outlaw in his degre,
Sic pardon got before a King,
As did the Outlaw Murray of the Foreste frie?

Hangingshaw Castle appears to have been destroyed by fire around 1760 along with many records of early life in Ettricke. George Burnett in his *Companion to the Tweed*, published in 1938, states that Hanginshaw was once held by local inhabitants to be 'the largest and the best, the richest and the grandest house in the south of Scotland'. A style of living said to have begun in the days of Outlaw Murray, was carried on down through the centuries including the custom that all visitors must drink a quart pot of Haningshaw ale in one draught. Before leaving the Murrays it must be noted that a plaque in the Murray Aisle of Selkirk's Kirk of the Forest records the following: 'In the Murray aisle of the present building lie the maternal ancestors of Franklin D Roosevelt, 32nd President of the USA.'

Broadmeadows, where the first youth hostel in Scotland was established, and still flourishes, was the scene of the murder of Sir William Douglas the 'dark Knight of Liddesdale'.

Already mentioned in the chapter on Liddesdale, Sir William was murdered by his godson the Earl Douglas; as Scott puts it, 'upon a jealousy that the Earl had conceived of him with his lady'.

It would be easy to miss Yarrow Kirk in its screen of trees, just opposite where a minor road bridges the Yarrow to cross into the Ettrick Valley. This is the replacement for the 'Forest Kirk' or 'St Mary's of the Lowes' which stood very much in the west of the parish overlooking St Mary's Loch. Built on Buccleuch property in 1640, during the time of the National Covenant, the original building was constructed in the austere style of the times. Walls were only thirteen feet high; the floor was beaten earth and while the roof was slated rather than thatched, this was open to the interior of the building.

What we see as Yarrow Kirk today is much altered from this early period, although the cross-shaped plan remains as in the original. In 1772 the walls were raised by some three feet and galleries installed and so improvements have continued. Eventually the galleries were removed and doors were added to the pews for the restraint of the sheepdogs which seemingly attended services with their masters. Windows were enlarged or installed while a disastrous fire in 1922 left only the bare walls standing, destroying the old Communion vessels and the brass plaques commemorating the names of the famous who were associated with Yarrow Kirk. These included Sir Walter Scott, who had been a regular attender when living at Ashestiel which was in the parish.

Some items were saved including the bell dated 1657 and the sundial on the south-west corner bearing the message, 'Watch and Pray / Tyme is Short'. Mellow oak is used in much of the interior woodwork; light blue paint in places along with stained glass windows make the modern-day Yarrow Kirk a far cry from the stark basic building of the Covenanters.

Nearby on the road west can be seen the two most conspicuous of the Yarrow Stones associated with the Dowie Dens Ballad, although a small standing stone near the kirkyard gate is said also to have associations. The first significant stone is seen shortly after passing the Yarrow War Memorial where soon on the right it stands some fifty yards from the road within a small field enclosed by dry stone dykes. The other, the inscribed stone fenced against stock damage, lies half a mile farther on beside the track to Whitfield farm.

Writing in the 1833 Statistical Account, Dr Robert Russel, the Yarrow minister, gives this account of the stones, while placing their origin centuries before the ballad incident.

There is a piece of ground lying to the west of Yarrow Kirk, which appears to have been the scene of slaughter and sepulchre. From time immemorial it was a low, waste moor, till twenty-five years ago when formed into a number of cultivated enclosures. On more than twenty spots were large cairns, in many of which fine yellow dust, and in one an old spear was found. Two unhewn, massive stones still stand about one hundred yards distant from each other, and which, doubtless are monuments of the dead. The real tradition simply bears that here a deadly feud was settled by dint of arms; the upright stones mark the spot where the two lords or leaders fell, and the bodies of their followers were thrown into a marshy pool called the Dead Lake in the adjoining haugh. It is probable that this is the locality of the 'Dowie Dens of Yarrow.'

An opinion shared in the *History of the Berwickshire Naturalists' club*, here the site is also given as a burial ground for the early people of the Forest. Numerous human remains have been found around the site of the Yarrow Stone(s), including cist burials. Artifacts uncovered include bronze axe heads, pottery and flint tools. When breaking in the ground for a garden the shepherd of Warriors Rest cottage is said to have uncovered several of these cists, the bones within crumbling to dust when the air reached them. As these tombs are said to lie in an east-west direction there is a suggestion here that these were burials of people converted to the Christian religion. In fact so numerous were the human bones below some of the cairns that a witness reports that early in the nineteenth century 'the *old* Dr Russel carted them off to use as fertiliser in his Glebe'.

The inscribed Yarrow Stone is said to bear, or to have borne, a scratched rather than carved Latin inscription, which has been the subject of much debate since it was allegedly uncovered by the plough during the reclaiming operation mentioned above. Below it were found quantities of bones and ashes. Possibly the Yarrow Stone dates from around the fifth or sixth century and certainly to the untrained eye there remains little trace of any lettering upon its surface today.

One of the major Yarrow Stones; the other can just be discerned in the distance at the bend in the farm track.

One translation of the inscription by Craig Brown, author of *Selkirkshire*, goes thus:

> Here is the monument of Cetilous and Nennus, sons of Dumnonium prince and emperor. Here lie buried the two sons of Liberalis.

An alternative, again from the Berwickshire Naturalists is.

> This is the sepulchre of Catellus and Finn, sons of the illustrious Nudd, chief of the Dummonians. Here lie in the tomb the two sons of Hael.

One thing is certain: the Yarrow Stones may have been the site of the duel, or a convenient site to place the event, but they predate the ongauns between the two Scott families by ten centuries or more.

Back to the ballad which, due to the sheer number of lairds bearing the name Scott, has caused some confusion in the past. Sir Walter Scott first thought that the story concerned the murder of John Scott, sixth son of the Laird of Harden, by the Scotts of Gilmanscleugh. Later he thought it equally possible that the fight was between John Scott of Tushielaw and his brother-in-law, Walter Scott, third son of Robert Scott of Thirlestane, in which the latter was killed. Selkirk Presbytery records (Feb 7th 1609) reveal that John Scott of Tushielaw faced excommunication for the murder of Walter Scott of Thirlestane.

So, if the ballad is to be believed, here on the north bank of the Yarrow two Border families of Scotts came to settle the matter over land which the Tushielaw Scott conveyed or intended to convey to his daughter upon her marriage to Scott of Thirlestane. Even in Sir Walter Scott's time different versions of this ballad were in existence and other ballad collectors disagreed with Scott's version, saying that the true version had 'Yarrow' in each verse and that the lady was Grizel and not Sarah.

Scholars will doubtless continue to disagree upon the origins of this ballad; perhaps it is better to enjoy the words and story rather than argue about their origins. The version given by William Aytoun in *The Ballads of Scotland* sounds as good as any and not unusually for a bloody tale, this version starts with a drinking bout.

> Three lords were birling at the wine,
> On the Dowie dens o' Yarrow;
> They set a combat them among,
> To fight it on the morrow.

> You took our sister to be your wife,
> And thought her not your marrow,
> You stole her frae her father's back,
> When she was the Rose o' Yarrow.

The duel is arranged for the following day — strange how these Ettrick lairds decided to settle their differences in the neighbouring valley instead of on their home ground. Off goes the hero, hair combed by the good lady, sword at side, to the dowie dens where instead of the knight he expected to meet in single combat:

> As he gaed up the Tinnis bank,
> I wot he gaed wi' sorrow;
> It's there he spied nine armed men,
> On the dowie dens o' Yarrow.

O come ye here to hawk or hound,
Or drink the wine sae clear, O?
Or come ye here to part your land,
On the dowie dens o' Yarrow?

In the desperate fight the hero wounds four of his adversaries and kills five before he himself is slain by a cruel blow from behind by the lady's brother.

Gae hame, gae hame, my brother John,
What needs this dule and sorrow?
Gae hame and tell my lady dear,
That I sleep sound on Yarrow.

A further ballad, 'Willie's Drowned in Yarrow', confuses the issue, being of the same measure as 'The Dowie Dens of Yarrow' and so making it possible for reciters to mix the two incidents.

Willie's rare and Willie's fair,
And Willie's wondrous bonny,
And Willie's hecht to marry me,
Gin e'er he married ony.

She sought him east, she sought him west,
She sought him braid and narrow;
Syne, in the cleaving of a craig
She fand him drowned in Yarrow.

Above Yarrow the Southern Upland Way wends its course from Innerleithen by the old Minch Moor road used by Montrose in his flight from Philiphaugh. An earthwork between Peat Law and Snouthead known as the Wallace Trench sits astride two ancient ridge roads. It is uncertain whether this was constructed or merely utilised by the patriot prior to the battle of Stirling Brig.

The uplands between the valleys of Tweed and Yarrow, Yarrow and Ettrick and Ettrick and Teviot make for excellent walking; the Southern Upland Way is but one route which wends by Ettrick, Yarrow and then Tweed. Old hill tracks can be found, suitable for the all-terrain or mountain bike, rising and falling from river valley to river valley. Even the motorist can thread his way through the four valleys by B and unclassified roads, where from the comfort of the driving seat away from the red lines on the map it is possible to discover parts of the Borders well away from the normal tourist trails. Soon we encounter Yarrow's first associations with James Hogg, the shepherd poet and friend of Scott, who, although he spent much of his life farming in Yarrow, is more familiar as The Ettrick Shepherd from his own choice of pen name. Hogg came from a similar rural background to Burns, of whom he was an admirer but lacked the education afforded to Burns; the Ettrick Shepherd had only some six months' official schooling. It was Hogg's mother, born Margaret Laidlaw, who coached Hogg both in the art of reading and equally important in the lore and legend of the Borders — tales imprinted deep in his memory from earliest days.

James Hogg's shepherding life began when he was six years old for the reward of a ewe lamb and a pair of shoes for the half year. By the age of fifteen he had worked for a dozen employers, always leaving to improve his wage or fee. But was his early life one of drudgery and toil? If it were how could he possibly have written:

> Where the pools are bright and deep,
> Where the grey trout lies asleep,
> Up the river and o'er the lea,
> That's the way for Billy and me.

Was that an account of an early boyhood fishing expedition or was it wistful thinking for what he had missed? He worked up and down the valleys of Ettrick and Yarrow including a period on Yarrow at Blackhouse where, when working for the Laidlaw family, his education continued and his early attempts at writing were encouraged.

Eventually as his parent's health failed James Hogg returned to Ettrickhall where he had his first meeting with Sir Walter Scott, who was brought by Willie Laidlaw from Blackhouse where he had arrived in search of Hogg. Sir Walter had become aware of James Hogg when the latter's first book of verse was published in 1801. In Hogg's own opinion in later years this was mediocre but thanks to its publication it brought together two of the Borders' most prominent writers of the age. Both James Hogg and Willie Laidlaw were among the many people who assisted Scott in the collection of Border ballads.

Scott and Hogg of course went on to write extensively, basing many of their stories upon the Borders. Will Laidlaw ended his days as steward at Abbotsford, his only well-known contribution to literature being the poem 'Lucy's Flitting', a term you still hear used today to describe a house or a room in a turmoil — stated perhaps something like this, 'aye but the place was fair upside doon, a right steerie jist like Lucy's flittin'.

Although they came from entirely different backgrounds, Scott and Hogg remained friends for life even if sometimes the relationship was a mite stormy when Hogg, a somewhat vain man by all accounts, imagined some slight. At their first meeting at Ettrickhall, Hogg's mother is said to have given Scott his first rendering of 'Auld Maitland'. Enquiring of the old lady as to whether this ballad had ever been printed before she is said to have replied, 'Oh, na, sir, there were never any o' my sangs prenit till ye prenit them  yoursel', an' ye hae spoilt them athegither. They were made for singin, an' no for reading; but ye hae broken the charm now, an' they'll never be sung mair. An' the worst thing o' a' they're neither right spell'd nor right settin doun.'

Prominent figures in the world of literature such as Byron, Wordsworth and the Brontes all regarded Hogg as a leading writer of the time; it was only after his death that critics began to deride the work of the Ettrick Shepherd. When a slump hit the sheep trade early in the nineteenth century Hogg resolved to seek his fortune in the world of publishing, setting out for Edinburgh in 1810 to pursue this aim. For various reasons Hogg's weekly literary magazine, *The Spy*, only lasted a year resulting in his return to the Borders.

Today there is a revival of interest in the work of the Ettrick Shepherd, his *Confessions of a Justified Sinner* being considered by academics today a work of fiction far before its time. 'Lock the door, Lariston' makes a stirring Border ballad, while his 'Kilmeny from the Queen's Wake' must rank at least equal to any verse in the English language and tells of a young girl vanished temporarily into a promised land.

A land where sin had never been;
A land of love and a land of light.

When seven long years had come and fled:
When grief was calm and hope was dead;
When scarce was remembered Kilmeny's name,
Late, late in the gloaming Kilmeny came hame!

Many of Hogg's works dealt with the supernatural, where of course he had a distinct advantage in his maternal grandfather, William Laidlaw, who, as his tombstone records, was 'The far famed Will o' Phaup, Who for feats of Frolic, Agility and Strength Had no Equal in his day'. Will o' Phaup was born in 1691 being, on his own claim, the last person in the south of Scotland to converse directly with the fairies. Or was it a late return from a market day which brought on the claim — Will's memory clouded by the dealings of the day? We must only surmise that Will believed it and the story was then passed down through two generations to his grandson.

Unlike Burns, Hogg never aspired to the habits of upper-class society especially that of Edinburgh, always being content to be the Ettrick Shepherd in dress and manners. A much prized offer of a seat to attend the coronation of George IV, obtained for him by Scott, was turned down as the date clashed with St Boswell's Fair and it would have been unseemly for Hogg as a new tenant farmer to have missed the most important event in the Border calendar.

Hogg did visit London in 1832 where he was fêted by the literary establishment of the day; Carlyle describes his appearance before continuing: 'I felt interest for the poor "herd body"; wondered to see him blown hither from his sheepfolds, and how, quite friendless as he was, he went along, cheerful, mirthful and musical.' Hogg died in November 1835. His remains rest in Ettrick alongside those of his parents and close by to Tibbie Shiels, the most famous innkeeper of Border history.

From Blackhouse Heights several small streams unite to form the Douglas Burn at Blackhouse where Hogg worked for the Laidlaws. Here between the farm house and a cottage stands the ruin of Blackhouse Tower, where is said to have

Remains of Douglas Tower

been one of the first grants of land to the Black Douglas family who for centuries played a major role in the shaping of Scottish history.

Two miles from the Yarrow Road, Blackhouse is touched by the Southern Upland Way en route from Dryhope on the east end of St Mary's Loch to Innerleithen. According to Godscroft this was the baronial seat of the Douglases in the time of Malcolm Canmore, a son of the first Lord Douglas having attended a Scottish parliament held at Forfar. The Tower, where lived perhaps Robert the Bruce's good Sir James, is but a ruin, crumbled to scarce one storey high. Square with a circular stairway, there could have been little comfort for the Douglas family within the walls of unworked stone. Not that this would have mattered to the Douglas with a motto 'better to hear the lark sing than the mouse cheep'.

This is also the setting for the ballad 'The Douglas Tragedy', which somehow has a familiar ring; a handsome young man courting a beautiful maiden whose family did not approve of the liaison. The young man, Lord William in the ballad, was not put off by his lady's parental disapproval, eloping with Lady Margaret north towards Peebles with her father and seven stout brothers in pursuit. A circle of eleven stones, some still standing, but of much greater antiquity than the ballad, are said to mark the place where Lady Margaret's father and brothers caught up with the lovers.

Here Lady Margaret:

> Held his steed in her milk white hand,
> And never shed one tear,
> Until she saw her seven brethern fa',
> And her father hard fighting, who loved her so dear.

Lord William despatches his lover's family before the pair continue on their flight where, on stopping to take a drink from a burn, it is apparent that William is sorely wounded.

> O they rade on, and on they rade,
> And a' by the light of the moon,
> Until they came to yon wan water,
> And there they lighted doon.
>
> They lighted down to take a drink
> Of the spring that ran sae clear;
> And down the stream ran his guid heart's blood,
> And sair she began tae fear.

By morning Lord William has died from his wounds and Lady Margaret from a broken heart. They are laid to rest in St Mary's kirkyard overlooking the loch, where eventually the rose and briar which grow from their respective graves meet and entwine, joining together forever the lovers in death.

> Lord William was buried in St Marie's Kirk,
> Lady Marg'ret in Mary's quire;
> Out o' the lady's grave grew a bonny red rose,
> And out o' the knight's a brier.
>
> And they twa met, and then they plat,
> And fain they would be near;
> And a' the world might ken right weel
> They were twa lovers dear.
>
> But bye and rade the Black Douglas,
> And wow but he was rough!
> For he pull'd up the bonny brier,
> And flang'd in St Marie's Loch.

St Mary's is the final scene for another ballad of a Scottish

Borderer whose love lived in England; again the relationship is
forbidden by her parents but on this occasion for some reason
the hero does not ride out and simply abduct the lady. Instead
they exchange messages with a Gay Goss-Hawk which seems to
have all the attributes of a homing pigeon.

> O Well is me, my gat goss-hawk,
> That ye can speak and flee;
> For ye shall carry a love-letter
> To my true love frae me.

Lord William and his lady carry out a comprehensive correspondence by the faithful bird, hatching a plot to have the lady
brought to Scotland. If she is not alive to marry Lord William,
she requests her father to at least, 'In Scotland bury me'.
Dropping down in a swoon, which is all part of the plot, the
heroine is to all intents and purposes dead. An auld witch wife
of the household is suspicious, giving instructions to drop
molten lead on her face to see if in fact she is dead.

> An drap it on her rose-red lips,
> And she will speak again;
> O meikle will a maiden do,
> To her true love to win!

Despite this horror the ruse is successful and the lady is
enclosed in a bier made by her seven brothers, within a shroud
sewn by her seven sisters before the cortège sets out for the fourth
kirk in Scotland, St Mary's, where she desires to be buried, after
tolling bells, saying mass and paying gold at the first three kirks.

> But when they cam to St Mary's kirk,
> There stude spearmen all on a raw;
> And up and started Lord William,
> The chieftane amang them a'.

On their arrival Lord William desires one last look at his fair
love's face, whereupon she springs to life telling her seven
brothers to 'Gae hame and blaw your horn'.

'I cam' not here to fair Scotland,
To lie among the dead;
But I cam' here to fair Scotland,
Wi' my ain true-love to wed.'

Perhaps it was at St Mary's, also known as the 'Forest Kirk', that Wallace was chosen as Guardian of Scotland. Already we have seen the present-day Yarrow Kirk further down the valley, the final demise of St Mary's accelerated by a party of Scotts led by Lady Buccleuch who sacked the building in 1557 during a feud with the Cranstoun family.

Of St Mary's of the Lowes nothing remains but the stone-walled burial ground on a flat shelf of land, a stiff ten-minute climb from the lochside road; the path is signposted and there is some parking space. The situation is superb, even if it is exposed and windswept, with views west along the loch and east into the Yarrow valley. Headstones still stand within the old kirkyard including an ornate sepulchre to the Bryden family. Many of the grave markers are just that, mere slabs of unworked stone set in the earth among the green mounds apparently devoid of inscription or carving.

This was the land of the Covenanters, the adherents to a religious principle who would not waver in the face of persecution, torture or death. Hiding among the hills these bands would conduct their own religious services in the manner they thought fitting. To commemorate their strength of will and privations a service known as the Blanket Preaching is held each year in August at St Mary's Kirk.

Between St Mary's and Craig Douglas, set back a little from the main road, stands the stumpy remains of Dryhope Tower, the birthplace of Marion Scott, known for her beauty as 'The Rose of Yarrow'. In 1576 Marion Scott married Walter Scott of Old Kirkhope in Ettrick, later known as Auld Wat of Harden, a Borderer famed at least in legend and ballad for his cattle stealing exploits. In fact it is said that part of the marriage contract required his father-in-law to maintain Harden for a year and a day, while he in turn undertook not to oust his wife's parents from their home.

One version of 'The Dowie Dens' ballad begins:

At Dryhope lived a lady fair,
The fairest flower in Yarrow,
And she refused nine noble men
For a servan' lad in Gala.

Was this then the lady who was responsible for the deeds at
Yarrow Stone in an episode of her life before she was courted
by Auld Wat, when he was yet young? Her father was an alleged
noted cattle thief in his own right, no doubt finding the wild
glens of Kirkstead and Dryhope burns ideal hiding places for
the cattle he borrowed from over the Border.

There remains a further ballad before we leave Yarrow —
'The Lament of the Border Widow' — dating from the expedition into the Borders of James V in his purge of law-breaking
clans. Tradition and the ballad record that Perys Cokburne of
Henderland was condemned and hanged over his own gate
leaving the sorrowing widow to bury her spouse.

There came a man, by middle day,
He spied his sport, and went away;
And brought the King that very night,
Who brak my bower, and slew my knight.

I took his body on my back,
And whiles I gaed, and whiles I sat;
I digg'd a grave, and laid him in,
And happ'd him wi the sod sae green.

'But think na ye my heart was sair,
When I laid the moul' on his yellow hair?
O think na ye my heart was wae,
When I turn'd about, away to gae.'

It was not Perys however but William Cockburn who was tried
at Edinburgh in 1530. He was convicted of treason as having
solicited the aid of Englishmen to rob his own neighbours, and
condemned to death by beheading. A grave on the site of the
old chapel of Henderland records that here lies 'Perys of
Cokburne and hys wyfe Marjory', the lettering on the broken
stone now impossible to read. Of Henderland Tower there is

only a pile of rubble and a traceable line of what was possibly the outer wall or barmiken. A short distance upstream on the Henderland Burn, a waterfall in a steep ravine, the Dow Glen, is known as the Lady's Seat where the lady is said to have mourned the loss of her spouse.

'Nae living man I'll love again,
Since that my lovely knight is slain,
Wi' ae lock o' his yellow hair
I'll chain my heart for evermair.'

From Henderland the road leads eventually to Tweedsmuir where among these hills are found three major water reservoirs supplying the city of Edinburgh and the Lothians. Talla was the first of these early this century but the most recent is Megget holding 64 million cubic metres. It was completed in the 1980s and in addition to the water retained by the dam also has water pumped from St Mary's Loch. Megget, with the existing reservoirs of Talla and Fruid, now form a trio of artificial lochs in the river valleys where the Ettrick Shepherd strode and fished the burns which now lie submerged.

Over and above being a water resource, these reservoirs also provide an amenity in that all are available for trout angling at a reasonable cost. Alongside Megget can be found five viewpoints and information sites which record the history of the valley prior to flooding. Here we learn that gold was once mined in the Ettrick Forest, enough to present Elizabeth I with a porringer in the late sixteenth century; some of the gold could well have come from the Megget Burn. Through Megget once run the Thief's Road and the Old Road, both of which were used as drove roads between the seventeenth and nineteenth centuries.

Cramalt, where one of the information and picnic sites can be found, once boasted two towers guarding this important crossing between the valleys of Yarrow and Tweed. It was not until the late 1970s that excavations revealed the fact that there two towers here, the existence of the south tower only being revealed at this time. The north tower is considered to have been built as an additional defence or to provide accommodation for James V on his business and pleasure outings among the Borderers. Once complete with pit prison and one of only

Megget reservoir; information boards and reconstructed tower base.

thirty such places of detention found in Scotland, the north tower was only surpassed in size in this part of the Borders by those of Neidpath and Newark. Now lying below forty metres of water, the ground floor plan and part of the wheelstair of the Cramalt's north tower have been rebuilt above the present level of Megget Water.

Of course no artificial water can match the natural, and so it is with St Mary's Loch. Set in an almost unspoiled situation where smooth round hills sweep down to the bank, the jewel of St Mary's is the largest of the natural lochs found in the Borders. Actually there are two lochs here, St Mary's and the smaller Loch of the Lowes, where on the strip of land between the two can be found Tibbie Shiel's — one of the most famous hostelries in Britain. It was named after the first proprietor, born Tibbie Shiel. She married Robert Richardson in 1813, but he unfortunately died in 1824, a year after moving to the then newly built cottage between the lochs. Left with six children, Tibbie took in as her first guest Robert Chambers, who was engaged in collecting material for his *Picture of Scotland*.

Chambers was fair taen on with the hospitality afforded at Tibbie's, paving the way for a host of nineteenth-century literary

Tibbie Shiel's Inn; meeting place for many 19th century writers.

figures who would grace the door of the little white house. Hogg described it as being as snug as a wren's nest, sitting on the crossroads of the old hill roads between Yarrow and Moffat, Ettrick and Tweed.

Hogg, a handsome man by any standards if the sculptor is to be believed, sits in stony pensive silence overlooking the picnic site at Oxcleuch. What he makes of the scene today we can only imagine, but it is worthwhile noting one of the quotations on his statue:

> At evening fall in lonesome dale,
> He kept strange converse with the gale,
> Held worldly pomp in high derision,
> And wandered in a world of vision.

Upstream of Loch of the Lowes the river Yarrow now becomes little Yarrow as it rises to the watershed with the Moffat Water; from here the Borders District boundary climbs to the high ridge, dividing the upper part of the Yarrow Valley from Ettrick.

To choose a favourite between the valleys of Yarrow and Ettrick is virtually impossible. Yarrow has its ballads and the

Over Phawhope, now an open bothy for hill walkers.

jewel of St Mary's Loch at its head; Ettrick on the other hand is unlike any of the other major river valleys dealt with in this book in that no motor road crosses its watershed. Tweed, Teviot, Yarrow and Gala Water all have their A roads running alongside; Ettrick does have two B roads running across it to Hawick and Langholm — splendid outings for the motorist — but to climb alongside Ettrick's source it is a case of Shank's pony. It is at Ettrick Head where the cross-country walking route, the Southern Upland Way, enters the Borders Region that the infant Ettrick is born between Capel Fell and Wind Fell at Over Phawhope where lived James Hogg's grandfather, Will o' Phaup.

Sitting on the edge of forestry the old shepherd's cottage of Over Phawhope is now maintained by the Mountain Bothies Association as an open bothy for walkers. From here the Southern Upland Way follows the Ettrick Water downstream to climb eventually by Scabcleugh Burn to Yarrow and Tibbie's. An excellent short outing of around four–five hours' duration sampling some of the Southern Uplands can be made here from where the public but unclassified road ends at Potburn (ample parking is available).

It is a simple matter of following the road first to Potburn, then Over Phawhope, now alongside the Entertrona Burn almost due east from the bothy, to climb the flank of Ettrick Pen leading to a cairn on the rounded top. The view is superb north-west to White Coomb and Lochcraig Head above Loch Skeen, then almost around the compass where the plantations of Eskdale and Craik Forests stretch unbroken into the distance. Navigation is no problem from Ettrick Pen to Ettrick Head, following a fence over Hopetoun Craig and Wind Fell to join the well-signed Southern Upland Way along a path, then forestry road, back to Over Phawhope.

The population in the Ettrick Valley is now downstream at Ettrickbridge; the old village of Ettrick is barely a handful of dwellings — the kirk, a primary school and a corrugated iron village hall. Once Ettrick was the property of the Napier family and the kirkyard bears witness to the generations of that name who are now but a memory. Back in the mists of time the earliest religious house in the upper Ettrick, perhaps only a monk's cell, can be found in the name of Over Kirkhope and Kirkhope Burn, not to be confused with Old Kirkhope at Ettrickbridge.

A monument to James Hogg can be found at Ettrickhall, a short distance upstream of Ettrick Village, while in the burial ground of Ettrick Kirk the Shepherd was laid to rest in 1835. It was at Ettrick Kirk that Thomas Boston, mentioned also in Borders 1, spent twenty-five years of his ministry. A strong adherent of the Covenanting principles, Boston's first Holy Communion at Ettrick saw fifty-seven participants. Eventually his renown throughout the upland area was such that twenty-one years later his Communion was the event of the year in this Border country, drawing seven hundred and seventy seven worshippers from the surrounding area.

Downstream a short distance lies Tushielaw where the tower was the stronghold of Adam Scott, who, in a country noted for robbers, was afforded the title 'King of Thieves'. As in the case of Cokburne of Henderland the popular legend is that Adam Scott was hanged from his own gallows tree in the same punitive expedition of James V. History records however that he did receive a trial and sentence and his severed head joined that of Cokburne's on Edinburgh Tollbooth following his execution.

Monument at the birthplace of James Hogg, the Ettrick Shepherd.

Standing high above the south bank of the Ettrick all that remains of the infamous robber's tower is a crumbling section of barrel vaulting on the ground floor; the remainder of the walls which appear to have been of undressed stone lie scattered around. Adam Scott is recorded as having his own gallows tree where summary treatment was dealt out to those who offended him. A stunted ash growing beside the ruins may have sprung from a seedling of this dreaded bough.

Before becoming Wat of Harden, then Auld Wat, Walter Scott

Remains of Tushielaw Tower. The simple but effective method of barrel vaulting can be easily seen.

no doubt set out on many a moonless night, perhaps by the track still shown skirting Sundown Height, to court and win the hand of Mary or Marion Scott when she was the 'Flower of Yarrow'. Wat's coat-of-arms is to be found on the bridge over the Ettrick at Ettrickbridgend — a construction Wat Scott is said to have been forced to erect as an act of penance for some misdeed.

Overlooking Ettrick stands the tower of Oakwood, or Aikwood, one of the best preserved of the old Border towers. It was Sir Walter Scott who placed the Wizard, Michael Scott, here — he who, among other deeds, is said to have cleft the Eildon Hills into three. There is some four hundred years' difference between Sir Walter and the time when Michael Scott lived, but the man was real, even if some of his deeds were exaggerated.

Oakwood Tower is one of the best preserved keeps to be found anywhere in the Borders, recently renovated into a family home by Borders M.P., Sir David Steel. Sir Walter Scott is generally held responsible for placing Oakwood Tower as the home of Micheal Scott the Wizard, known in Scotland and beyond four hundred years before Oakwood Tower was built.

Leaving the valleys of Ettrick and Yarrow can only be done with reluctance, the haunting air of ballad and mystery difficult to shake off. But leave we must if space is to remain to discover one of the Borders' oldest towns and the upper valley of the Tweed.

# CHAPTER 5

## *Selkirk*

Selkirk, a Royal and Ancient Burgh of Scotland, once the county town for the shire bearing its name, straggles uphill from Ettrick's banks to Selkirk Common. Burgh and county were swept aside in the local government reforms of 1975, ending in a stroke a long tradition of self-government for and by the Souters — as native-born citizens of the town are proud to be called. Souter or shoemaker was a traditional Selkirk craft dating back to the times when there was a plentiful supply of hides from the deer of Ettrick Forest. Early shoes were 'single-soaled shoon', sewn outside-in then turned about for wearing, something in the manner of a moccasin. Shoemakers are mentioned throughout Selkirk's history but the last working souter in the town retired in 1975.

It was here that Sir Walter Scott, under the patronage of the Duke of Buccleuch, was appointed Sheriff Depute of the County of Selkirk in December, 1799. A statue of Scott overlooks the square, although his political appointment to the post at the time was not necessarily met with approval by the townspeople. It might appear that Selkirk's connection with such a famous personality as Sir Walter Scott would be the most important incident in the town's history, yet it is but a recent event for the Royal and Ancient Burgh — a status confirmed by James V in 1535 by Royal Charter although the town had enjoyed at least Burgh status since the reign of King David I.

Settlement on the Ettrick banks dates from the Mesolithic site at Rink Farm, the earliest evidence of human occupation in the Selkirk area. Bronze-age man left little impact upon the land around Selkirk other than pottery shards and burial sites. Romans established a camp at Oakwood during their occupation and according to chroniclers the native Iron-age Celtic tribe, the Selgovae, even in the third century AD did not cultivate any land but lived by their flocks and hunting.

Following the departure of the Romans in the early fifth century the valleys were re-occupied by Celts, perhaps from

Berwickshire and the Lothians, who settled in the area until the seventh century when the Angles and Saxons spread their settlements upstream throughout the Tweed System.

Despite conflict with native peoples the Angles endured and were responsible for founding, and most likely giving Selkirk its name, translated as 'church in the wood'. Today there is no definite evidence of the true site of 'schelch'-'circe' but the triangular layout of the old town seems Anglian in origin. Whether the church came with the Angles or was a branch of the old Columban church is a matter of debate. Whatever its origin the scene was set for a Border town to play an important part in the history of Scotland, which of course only came into being in its present form when Malcolm II defeated the Northumbrians at the Battle of Carham in 1018.

Perched on the hillside above the Ettrick, old Selkirk occupies a situation that contrasts with its Border contemporaries which for the main part were founded in riverside situations. Development on Ettrick Haugh came later as the manufacture of cloth became industrialised, dependent first upon water-power to drive the early textile machinery.

When in the twelfth century Alexander I gave his brother David, Earl of Haddington, the greater part of southern Scotland, the way was open for the expansion of the Norman way of life north over the Border. Educated at the English court David was very much in favour of the feudal system introduced there by William the Conqueror. As the sixth son of Malcolm III David would never have expected to inherit the Scottish Crown but fate decreed otherwise and eventually in 1124 the pious David became King of Scots.

Prior to his ascension David had established his first Scottish religious house, the Tironensians at Selkirk, in 1113. The title of abbey as we know it may have been too grandiose for the humble building built by the thirteen monks of the Tironensian Order brought over from France. The Order was then only recently founded in 1109 in the Forest of Perche near Chartes, being an offshoot of the Benedictine Order and its members seeking a humbler way of life than that offered by their mother house.

Noted for their piety, the Trimonensians were reputedly also skilled artisans in building and metal working but just why

Selkirk was chosen for the first of Earl David's ventures into religious patronage is uncertain. A number of reasons are given by historians including the presence of David's castle at Selkirk and the similarity of the setting to their French mother house. Selkirk Abbey existed, if not actually flourished, for 15 years; the site is thought to have been that now occupied by the old burial ground at Lindean, downstream of Selkirk on the south bank of the Ettrick.

Four years after falling heir to the Scottish Crown in 1124, King David decided to move his Trimonensians to Kelso, near the Royal Castle of Roxburgh, his principal stronghold in the south of Scotland. The ruins of Kelso Abbey still stand magnificently overlooking the Tweed; the abbey was the forerunner of the quartet founded by King David. At the same time the extensive lands and privileges of Selkirk's Trimonensions were granted to the new house at Kelso. David, however, retained much of Selkirkshire as a royal hunting reserve, paving the way for the later establishment of Selkirk's Common Land.

Following the removal of the Trimonensians, Abbot's Selkirk also disappeared while the place we know as Selkirk today grew around the site of the early motte and bailey castle near the Haining Loch. Even so, this could have been a 'new town' replacing the earlier market town, perhaps Lauriston, with the possibility that even from the twelfth century Selkirk was granted royal status by King David in what seems to have been one of his favourite parts of Scotland.

The Scottish Wars of Independence brought English garrisons to Selkirk Castle and for a sixteen-year period it seems to have been continuously held by the English. In the spring of 1302 a programme of building ordered by King Edward I commenced, adding stone towers and a protective fence or pele in that year. By September 1302 the works were held up by a lack of timber for the roof, suggesting that despite being a forest area the woods around Selkirk were mainly scrubby. After being captured by the Scots, then retaken by English forces, the castle was eventually completed with wood taken from pontoons stored at Berwick.

In 1297 Sir William Wallace used Ettrick Forest as a safe haven before setting out to the famous Battle of Stirling Brig. Around this time (late 1297 to early 1298), Wallace was declared Guardian of Scotland but there is no definite proof if this occurred in the Selkirk area. An earthwork remains on Yarrow, still known as Wallace's Trench, which may have been part of an ancient boundary mark but was utilised by Wallace as a defence for the Scottish rebels' camp. During the period from 1297 until 1314 control of Ettrick Forest lay sometimes with the English and sometimes with the Scots. Power swayed back and forth with Sir James Douglas leading the home side; following Bannockburn the Forest of Ettrick was most likely granted to The Douglas in recognition of his contribution to the cause.

With such a wealth of history and tradition it is little wonder that one of Selkirk's songs — and there are several — goes thus:

> Auld Selkirk Toun's a bonnie toun,
> The favoured Forest Queen,
> The ancient haunt of Royalty,
> What splendour has been seen.
> The Souter dreams aboot the past in ages
> far awa,
> As he gangs up the New Road and doon
> the auld Back Raw.
>
> Chorus
>
> Auld Selkirk, auld Selkirk, she's ancient
> but she's braw,
> O' a' the bonnie Border touns, the fairest
> o' them a.

That is but one of the songs sung by the huge gathering of Souters when the Selkirk Common Riding is celebrated on the first Friday following the second Monday in June. Supported by up to 500 riders from aw the airts, the horseback cavalcade which follows the Selkirk Standard Bearer on the day is certainly the largest mounted event in the Borders, possibly the largest in Britain and certainly a spectacle worth seeing.

Why is Selkirk Common Riding such a popular event? Only one town in the Borders could be regarded as a rival, the much larger Hawick where a strictly male-only participation is allowed in the event. Selkirk has no such restriction and in addition to the ceremonial common boundary inspection there are other attractions on the day.

Fording Ettrick, Selkirk Common Riding, which is certainly one of the largest mounted festivals in Britain.

At many Border Festivals once the horse procession leaves the town there is little left for the rest of the citizens to do other than follow on by car, except perhaps to gather an excellent rose fertiliser from the streets. Not so at Selkirk; the foot procession led by the banners of the corporations or craft guilds play an equally important part in the day and over and above this there are no less than three bands in the town to keep a spring in the stride around Selkirk's steep streets and wynds. Playing a major part in the day's events is the Selkirk Silver Band who, since it replaced an earlier brass band in 1894, has featured in the Common Riding, assisted in more recent years by the Selkirk Pipe Band.

Somewhat smaller is the flute band whose duties begin at 4.00 a.m. with the Rouse Parade around the street to awaken the Standard Bearer and Provost for their day's duties. Shrill and sharp, even in the grey light of a damp June morning the flute band's stirring renditions of 'Jock o Hazeldean', 'Rowan Tree' and of course 'Auld Selkirk' echo from wall to wall of the old town. These are Scottish airs as you will hear them nowhere else and the beat of the snare drum recalls times when this was a true call to duty. Somehow, around 6.00 a.m. the flute band vanishes from the scene, having performed their unique vital role for another year's Common Riding.

At first only a small contingent follows the band, but it swells by the minute; parents come to the door with infants or hold them up at the window to see the procession pass. Older Souters look wistfully from the doorstep, perhaps remembering their own youth when they too were able to stride out behind the band. The Standard-Bearer's house is reached and the young man comes to join the band in a verse of 'Auld Selkirk' before the band is invited inside for refreshment.

Ever the crowd gathers, until by 6.45 a.m. the streets are filled from shop front to shop front with the Silver Band now in command. The Standard-Bearer is charged with his duties at a ceremony on the balcony of the Victoria Halls. A foot procession now heads for the Market Square, led by the Silver Band, with the banners of the Incorporations or Trades with their members and followed by Councillors and officials.

They proceed downhill to Ettrick's Banks, where led by the Standard-Bearer the cavalcade fords the river. Here at last the horses can be put to a gallop on the two-and-a-half-hour ride around part of the remnants of Selkirk Common, by Linglie Glen, Tibbie Tamson Grave to the summit of the Three Brethren to return to Shawburn Toll where the foot followers have dispersed, breakfasted, re-formed and marched to the Toll in anticipation of the Standard's safe return.

For many Border Burghs this would be the highlight of the day, the return of the flag, but for Selkirk this is but part of the proceedings. Before arriving there it may be opportune to have a look at what the Common Riding is all about. While the Trimonensians arrived at Selkirk in 1113, the foundation charter was not granted until 1120 when Selkirk Common is mentioned in official papers for the first time. In the 1535 Charter, Selkirk Common comprises some 11,200 acres, split almost evenly north and south of the town in roughly an hourglass shape, with Selkirk at the narrowest point.

Having originally been a royal common the ownership of rights upon it were contentious, individual adjoining landowners having been granted rights also at various times in addition to the burghers of Selkirk. All through the seventeenth century court cases ensued and even on some occasions the burghers rode out with the 'sound of drum', armed with hagbuts to drive offending livestock from what they considered to be their land.

Eventually in 1681 the Selkirk Common was divided by Act of Parliament, one of the first common lands to suffer this fate, when fourteen encroaching landowners shared in the bounty. Originally in all there were 34 miles of march or boundary, unmarked by hedge or wall but designated by cairns of stone or turf. Common land was an asset to any burgh where burghers had the right of pasturage and fuel collection; it was therefore an essential duty to inspect these boundaries on a regular basis to make sure all was in order. With one of the largest common lands in Scotland it is little wonder that Selkirk's neighbours cast covetous glances at this asset.

As a member of the convention of royal burghs in Scotland Selkirk was bound by a number of rules regarding the administration of the common; a £100 fine was imposed by the convention in 1601 for leasing common mills to the provost. A further fine came in 1603 when Selkirk failed to provide sufficient evidence to the convention that the marches had been ridden as decreed. Defending the common land even led to the murder of the provost, John Mithag, and bailie, James Keyne, by James Ker, Ralph Ker and William Renton, so the risks of protecting the burgh's rights could not be described as minimal.

Common land was much reduced following the 1681 decision, with a march more easily ridden, although the present-day ceremonial cavalcade only covers part of this. With the pressure of protecting boundaries now removed, the way was open for Common Riding to become a day of celebration, rather than an essential task. Charged with overseeing the boundary marking were the 'burleymen' or burgh law men assisted by younger attendants. It is easy to imagine how the seniors would delegate any hard work to the juniors while they themselves reposed at ease on a sun-warmed bank, perhaps with a dram or something similar.

Such was the way that Selkirk Common Riding was born, the proceedings being added to over the years. The trade guilds, bands and foot procession now wait at Shawburn to greet the Standard Bearer 'safe in'. The procession re-forms, those on foot and mounted heading for Market Place to the sound of 'The Flo'ers o' the Forest' and the final act of Common Riding day.

There are two songs entitled the 'Flowers of the Forest', both written by ladies — one by Mrs Cockburn of Fairnilee which is described as being sung to the tune of the 'Floo'ers o' the Forest'. Mrs Cockburn's version goes 'I've seen the smiling of Fortune beguiling' and this version is played as the procession heads back towards the Market Place. The other version (known for Selkirk Common Riding purposes as the 'Lament for Flodden', 'The Liltin', is played following a two-minute silence after the flag ceremony, towards which the procession from Shawburn Toll is now heading. This was written by Jean Elliot, daughter of the second baronet of Minto — 'I've heard them liltin' at the ewe-milkin'. It was written long after Flodden, of course. Some say that Jean Elliot's version was penned as the result of a wager with her brother Gilbert, in a challenge to write a ballad in traditional style and have it accepted as such.

Part of the Selkirk Common Riding commemorates the role played by the townsmen in the Battle of Flodden. As a Royal Burgh in the pyramid feudal system of owed allegiance, the burghers of Selkirk answered not to an overlord or baron but direct to the king when the call came to raise what was, after all, an amateur national army.

Deep rooted in Selkirk's Flodden legend is the story that, of the eighty men from the Royal Burgh who answered the call to arms, only one named Fletcher returned, bearing a captured English flag. So shocked was this sole survivor, that as the story goes, he was unable to reply when asked what had happened to the remainder, but instead cast the captured flag, scythe-like, in horizontal arcs, indicating that the remainder had fallen on the field of battle. By modern standards Selkirk was then but a small town with a total population of under 1000 but over 500; therefore, if the legend is true, a large proportion of the able-bodied men from Selkirk must have fallen.

This act of Fletcher's has long been incorporated into the Common Riding celebrations as the culmination of the day's events, although the Statistical Account mentions the flag from Flodden being carried, when riding the bounds, by a member of the Corporation of weavers.

There is no mention at that time of the flag-waving ceremony. The flag known as 'The Flodden Flag', with ribbons attached dating from 1748, is preserved in the town museum along with the sword said to have been carried by Brydon, the Town Clerk, on that fateful day. If this is the case it is obvious that more than

Casting the colours. The monument to Scott can be seen on the left-hand side of the photograph.

one Selkirk man survived; perhaps Fletcher was merely the first to return.

'Casting the Colours', as the ceremony is called, takes place upon a dais in Market Place, the surrounding area so packed with spectators that it would seem impossible for another person to fit in. The casting or flag waving, which may also have been introduced by Flemish weavers, is in itself a skilful operation moving the heavy cloth around in a now predetermined pattern in time to the Silver Band's playing. Seven flags are cast in the ceremony, that of the Royal and Ancient Burgh wielded by the Standard Bearer taking precedence over those of the Corporations, Colonial Society, Merchants and Ex Soldiers. Proceedings end with two minutes' silence followed by the playing of the 'Lament for Flodden', 'The Lilting'. Then finally on the dais the Burgh Flag is handed back, 'unsullied and untarnished', leaving the Souters free to spend the remainder of Common Riding Day on a lighter vein at the race meeting on Gala Rig.

The Burgh Flag carried by the Standard Bearer is, in Selkirk terms, a fairly new innovation dating only from 1805. At the previous year's event a disagreement between the council and the trades had led to the latter boycotting the ceremony when a merchant Robert Richardson became the first to bear and cast the flag on Common Riding Day.

During the Casting Ceremony the tune played before the dais by the Silver Band is 'The Souters of Selkirk', an air which is given two origins.

> Up wi the Souters o' Selkirk,
> And down wi' the fazart Lord Home,
> But up wi ilka braw callant
> That sews the single-soled shoon;
> And up wi the lads o' the Forest,
> That ne'er to the Southron wad yield,
> But diel scoup o' Home and his menzie,
> That stude sae abiegh on the field.

Some sources relate this song to the Battle of Flodden, where the Merse men under Home had in fact beaten the opposing wing of the English army, but were unable to assist the centre where the king was slain. Some historians discount this origin, claiming instead the incident was not Flodden but a rather vicious football match played on a haugh near Selkirk. This book is not going to enter into the pros and cons of either theory, but the football theory seems rather odd. Up until recent times the arranging of, and participation in such a football match would have been extremely difficult.

Fletcher is preserved for eternity, complete with flag, outside the Victoria Hall in a dramatic bronze statue by Border's sculptor, Thomas Clapperton. Come to think of it, Selkirk is a great place for statues; local writer, John Buchan Brown who wrote under the name of J.B. Selkirk, Mungo Park and Scott are all remembered in different materials.

Much of Selkirk's story, from the Stone Age to the present day, is told in Halliwell's House Museum, adjacent to Market Place. Preserved here is the Flodden Flag, Bryden's sword and many relics from everyday life; the site itself is said to have once been occupied by tanning pits.

Of the Corporations or Craft Guilds which take part in the colour casting, that of the Weavers is the oldest, dating from 1608. They were followed by the souters in 1609 and the tailors in 1610. It was not until much later that other trades followed

— the merchants' flag bears the date 1644, the fleshers were incorporated in 1679 and the hammermen in 1681. Each of the crafts had two representatives on the burgh council, a deacon and a colleague.

Part of a guild's function could be described today as quality control but it also sought to protect its members by restricting entry — the Incorporation of Weavers, for instance, had only twenty-two members two hundred years after being founded. At nearby Galashiels there were no such restraints and by 1777 there was a strongly supported Manufacturers Corporation there as weaving left behind its cottage industry image and moved into the industrial era.

As the banks of the Gala Water became crowded with mills, owners were only too glad to expand into Selkirk beside the Ettrick. The sites were feud out by public roup, each with access to the lade supplying water diverted from the Ettrick. The first mills were established here in the 1830s. Soon waterpower was insufficient for the demand placed upon it, even although in mills, such as one established at Philiphaugh, the steep-falling

Selkirk's Flodden Memorial.

Ettrick could produce 180 h.p., and eventually the first steam engines appeared in the 1840s.

Selkirk's new prosperity led to the building of the first turn-pike road from Gala in the 1830s. Twenty years later the railway carrying coal at cheaper rates arrived, relieving the Selkirk Mills from dependence upon the level of water in the Ettrick to drive spinning and weaving machinery. A ready supply of cheap coal made dying and drying of cloth much easier, allowing the manufacturers to indulge in new patterns and designs which were to become associated with the Selkirk Mills. From then on, as elsewhere in the woollen industry, production seemed to have reached its peak. In the late part of the nineteenth century the imposition of import duties by the U.S.A. caused one of the most serious slumps ever in the trade.

It was a pattern to be repeated through to the present day — industry at the whim of fashion. The popularity of knitwear hit the weaving industry, before it also succumbed to the public's choice of even more casual and lightweight clothes. Cloth is still woven in Selkirk; again it is quality rather than mass-market material and output now is but a shadow of what it was at its peak. The electronics industry has replaced some of the jobs formerly found in textiles while another major employer in the town, Selkirk Glass, turns out exquisite glass paperweights and other fancy goods.

On Ettrick Haugh some of the magnificent buildings raised to house the spinning and weaving industry now lie in disuse; some in fact are derelict. However, thanks to a grant from the European Commission, Scottish Borders Enterprise are set to embark on a programme of renovation.

Below Selkirk, on the left bank of the Ettrick, the Battle of Philiphaugh was fought in 1645 with the ferocity so common in religious conflicts. An army of Royalists under Montrose, including a number of Irish and their camp followers, had encamped at Philiphaugh after marching from Kelso and Jedburgh. Despite his army being only a thousand strong Montrose must have felt fairly secure, as he himself spent the night in Selkirk, mainly engaged in writing despatches, we are told, to Charles I.

David Leslie meantime, in command of a Covenanting army six times greater than the Royalist force, had marched down Gala Water and was in the hamlet of Sunderland Hall by

Magnificent industrial building of Ettrick and Yarrow Spinners, Ettrick Haugh, Selkirk.

midnight on September 12th. Leslie split his army into two parts, attacking Montrose's dug-in forces while early morning mist yet shrouded the haugh.

Surprised and outnumbered the Royalists were soon overwhelmed, despite Montrose with a small troop of horse making a desperate foray against the Covenanters. Persuaded by his friends that it was better to leave the field to maintain the king's cause than to fight to the death, Montrose began his flight which would end eventually on the scaffold at Edinburgh. No quarter, if any was promised, was accorded to the remainder of the Royalist army which had surrendered; camp followers — men, women and children — are said to have been cruelly butchered on the field or within the courtyard of Newark Tower. A covenanting minister present is said to have commented that 'This wark gaes bonnilie on!'

The final verse of the ballad 'The Battle of Philiphaugh' echoes these sentiments.

> Then let us a' for Lesly pray,
> And his brave company!
> For thae hae vanquish'd great Montrose,
> Our cruel enemy.

Somewhere during his flight from Philiphaugh north across the Minch Moor towards Peebles, Montrose and the money chest from which he would have payed his army parted company. Some stories relate it being thrown into a well or bog to prevent it falling into Leslie's hands. If anyone has found it since then no one is letting on.

Selkirk is the final, in fact the only major town on Ettrick's banks, upstream in this and the Yarrow Valley are only a few hamlets, farmsteads and, of course, St Mary's Loch, dealt with in an earlier chapter.

# CHAPTER 6

## Galashiels and Abbotsford

Just upstream of where the Gala Water joins the Tweed, one of the Border's major town, Galashiels, sits astride this tributary stream. Most usually termed Gala or Galy locally, the town's abbreviated name makes an easier mouthful than the full title for fellow Borderers. Settlement on the site of modern Galashiels dates back to at least the ninth century, the name itself based upon two, perhaps three, separate language sources. Gala is derived from Gwala, an old British word meaning 'the full stream' or the Welsh word Gal meaning 'scattered'; Shiels is a Saxon word for shelter. Depending upon which source is chosen Galashiels could be taken to mean either 'the shelters beside the full stream' or the 'scattered shiels' or huts.

Shiels is commonly used in a second syllable around Galashiels; a few miles up Gala Water can be found the farms of Over, upper or higher Shiels, and Nether Shiels, the lower settlement. Two Pictish Brochs at Torwoodlee and Bow Castle overlook the lower reaches of the Gala Water, while Glendearg beside the Allan Water indicates a place named by a people in possession long before the Germanic tribes forged their way into the Tweed valley.

The old Anglian Galashiels did not sit in the centre of the present-day town; rather it stood high above the Gala Water in a double row of houses either side of what is now Church Street. This appears to have been the centre of Galashiels right up to 1599, when, upon being created a Burgh of Barony, the town cross was erected on what must have been the village green. Modern plaques on the cross base dating from the 1930s commemorate the marriage of James IV to Margaret Tudor of England.

It was near here that the Act of Sasine, the granting of legal possession of feudal property, took place in 1502 or 1503 when John Murray, Sheriff of Selkirkshire, met with Margaret Tudor's attorney. This Act, the gift of the Lands of Ettrick Forest by James IV to his bride, or rather the marriage it marked, should

115

have seen the blossoming of a new era of peace in the Borders. Unfortunately this was not the case and alliances with the French crown led James to Flodden Field and death. A hundred years were to pass before a Stewart king ruled in England.

Witnesses to the ceremony included Scott of Buccleuch and William Hoppringle of Torwoodlee. The latter's descendants (now Pringles) still grant the right of cutting sod and taking a stone from the old tower of Torwoodlee for the symbolic re-enactment of the ceremony during Braw Lads Week.

Nearby at the junction of Gala Terrace and Scott Crescent was the site of an Anglo-Norman motte, a house which stood here being known as the 'Mote House' up until the end of the last century. At the east end of Church Street stands the sole remains of the old parish kirk in the shape of the Gala Aisle, or Scott Aisle as it is also known. The kirk which once stood here dated from 1617 while the Scott Aisle was added by Hugh Scott, the laird, in 1636 as a burial aisle.

Ruinous and neglected for many years the Scott Aisle has been subject to recent restoration complete with stone-flagged roof, in a project organised by the Ettrick and Lauderdale District Council. In the old burial ground surrounding Gala

The recently restored Scott Aisle, Gala.

Aisle are found gravestones dating from the 1600s and the family tomb and memorial to Mungo Park, the African explorer. A useful guide for the 'Galashiels Old Town Walk' is available in the town, the route being assisted by plaques at the sites of interest described above.

Little is known about the life in early Galashiels but by medieval times, in 1457 to be precise, the Pringles or Hoppringills received a grant of land in 'Gallowscheillis' and Misilee from their feudal superior, the Earl of Douglas. It was Andrew Hoppringill who in 1583 built a small tower in the town as a replacement for a previous building. Today Old Gala House, as it is known, is the oldest building in Galashiels.

Built as a secure peel with the main entrance on the first floor, Andrew Hoppringill's original tower still survives among the later additions to Old Gala House. As the Hoppringill's main family seat at the time lay at Smailholm, it could be assumed that originally this would be a second residence with little thought given for the comfort of the inhabitants. It also suggests that the town was now assuming some importance as a market and centre of commerce; otherwise why did the Hoppringill family find it necessary to have a residence here when at Smailholm they had a perfectly adequate home — unless it was for the purpose of collecting rents or feus, as by 1582 a settlement was developing along the Gala Water with three waulkmills and ten cornmills clustered along the lower banks. While these were owned by the laird Andrew Hoppringill, most were tenanted by inhabitants of Galashiels indicating that by this time the population of the village was on the increase.

Following the death of Andrew Hoppringill in 1586, his son James was declared heir to the estate from the Tollbooth at Selkirk. This young man must have had considerable influence, frequently attending the Royal Court of James VI in Edinburgh — so much so that by 1599 he was able to create Galashiels a Burgh of Barony with a weekly Wednesday Market plus an annual Midsummer's Fair. This expanded the prosperity of Galashiels, and that of James Hoppringill, who was knighted in 1610 to become thereafter Sir James Pringill. The following year the Pringle family (the name spelling appears to have changed around this time), opted for Galashiels as their principal place of residence, erecting a second building alongside but not connected to the original peel.

A visitor in the 1620s describes the meal enjoyed at Old Gala House, 'big pottage, long kale, bowe or white kale, which is cabbage, 'breoh sopps, powdered beef, roast and boiled mutton, a venison pie in the form of an egg, goose, then cheese and apples'. Quite a repast, perhaps reflecting the laird's lavish lifestyle which, combined with being created Justice of the Peace and standing surety for large sums of money, led to his financial downfall. Debts were such that by 1632 Sir James was forced to sell the lands of Gallowscheillis and Mosilee to his son-in-law, Hugh Scott of Deuchar. As a Borderer Hugh Scott had an impeccable pedigree; he was the son of 'Auld Wat o Harden' and his mother was Mary Scott, the celebrated 'Flower of Yarrow'. — A line of descent claimed also by Sir Walter Scott.

After the death of Sir James Pringle in 1635 the Scotts were now lairds of Gala and Hugh and Jean took up residence in the Old Gala House. Among the improvements of the time was the decoration of the ceiling to commemorate the event and it can still be seen today. By 1700 Sir James Scott was the 4th Scott Laird of Gala, being also M.P. for Roxburghshire. As did successive Scotts over the years, he carried out improvements including adding Georgian wings. It was the 8th Laird John Scott, a great friend of Sir Walter, who perhaps under the poet's romantic influence added the neo-Gothic towers.

Through the eighteenth and into the nineteenth century the Scott Lairds of Gala continued to assist in the development of industry in the town, granting leases at favourable rates to any inhabitants who wished to become established or expand in the textile industry. A new family home, New Gala House, was built by Major Hugh Scott in 1876. Nothing remains of the new residence which was demolished in 1985, while the Old House remains today four square and strong, despite four centuries of Border wind and weather.

The ownership of Old Gala House has passed today to the Ettrick and Lauderdale District Council through a number of owners, including Galashiels Arts Club and Galashiels Town Council. In 1988 the District Council embarked upon a programme of renovation targeted at converting Old Gala House into a museum of local life, exhibition rooms and a meeting centre. Their aim has been precise; set among pleasant gardens a short distance from the town centre, the building now serves a useful function for both local inhabitants and visitors alike. Exhibition rooms provide space for artists and craftsmen to

One of Clapperton's best-known works in the Borders is the Galashiels War Memorial.

portray their skills, displays being changed on a monthly basis. The Museum Room, like the Laird's Room sited in the old tower, has an ongoing programme of themes ranging from natural history to how life was lived in Galashiels during the Second World War.

Galashiels-born sculptor, Thomas Clapperton (1879–1962), may not be well known outside his native town, yet his work can be seen throughout Britain from Edinburgh and Glasgow to Cardiff and London. Born at Bridge Street in Gala, Clapperton studied first at the Galashiels Mechanics Institute before completing his training in Glasgow and London. His best work perhaps remains in the Borders, including Selkirk's Flodden Memorial and the Border Reiver centrepiece of the Galashiels 1914–1918 war memorial. His work also features in war memorials throughout the Borders from Canonbie to Earlston. Within the Clapperton Room at Old Gala House are smaller examples of his work and an account of his life.

Galashiels Old Town Walk takes in, among other things, those places mentioned above and guides the visitor's footsteps to the premises of Peter Anderson and Co., where the firm which celebrated its centenary in 1992, maintains a museum on Galashiels and the tweed industry. Within the museum the story of cloth manufacture is told from its early beginnings right up to the present-day, from a simple homespun craft industry to one which, at least where Peter Anderson and Co. are concerned, caters for the very top end of the market in luxury cloth.

Although weaving must have already been carried out at Gala for many years it was only in 1666 that the participants banded together to form 'The Weavers' Corporation'. With a motto 'Weave Truth With Trust', members of the Corporation had a number of obligations including the full training of apprentices in the craft; failure to comply incurred a fine of £10. For almost two hundred years the Weavers' Corporation's influence was felt in Gala's weaving industry but by the mid-nineteenth century it was on the wane and the industrial revolution replaced the craft trade with a mechanised commercial enterprise. The last recorded meeting of the Corporation was held on 20th September 1847; their banner can still be seen in the Peter Anderson museum.

As the Weavers' Corporation declined there arose in its place the Manufacturers' Corporation, founded by ten mill owners in 1777 and still in existence to this day. Somehow the original flag of the Manufacturers was accidentally destroyed at one of the annual Michaelmas Day dinners (a story to be found here somewhere). The original's replacement, identical to that of the dyers' guild, also hangs in the Peter Anderson museum bearing the motto 'We Dye to Live and Live to Dye' — eight words which modern marketing consultants would find hard to surpass.

Meetings of the Manufacturers' Corporation are still held several times a year, where the colours and patterns likely to be in fashion in the next year are discussed in an attempt to gauge the mood of the future market. Galashiels and tweed cloth, of course, go hand in hand in many people's minds; along the banks of Gala Water as the Industrial Revolution mechanised the woollen industry, business soared and flourished. The troughs of national and international depression were also experienced with the ever changing fad of fashion always at hand to create financial disaster and unemployment.

Among the Border towns it would be difficult to put forward any one above the rest as a leader in the woollen industry; the writer for one is not brave enough to try. Most towns associated with the trade had their part to play. It would, however, be fair to say that the Gala manufacturers led the way in refining an already developed process in their fight for excellence in the end product.

Wool had for many years been a product of the Borderland, much of it exported to Flanders by the abbots of Melrose. Exporting raw fleeces had proved a valuable trade from around the founding of the abbeys up to the sixteenth century. Now it was seen as poor commercial practice when more revenue could be generated by producing yarn and cloth. Whether the aspect of work opportunity was recognised in these times is unknown. The English Parliament had been aware of the need for home manufacture before this was appreciated in Scotland; here those employed in the process of cloth production were exempt from taxation while finished cloth could be exported free of custom duties.

This course was followed in Scotland from the middle of the

seventeenth century with financial grants and special laws to assist the burgeoning trade. This even extended to a special decree by the Scots Parliament, demanding that the dead should now be buried in woollen cloth rather than the Scots linen, as had previously been the law. Special status for masters and workers in the industry gave them exemption not only from military service, but also from having troops quartered with them.

A coarse cloth, 'Galashiels Grey's' was woven at the time from local wool, well impregnated with tar while on the back of its rightful owner. At the annual Michaelmas Dinner of the Manufacturers' Corporation of Galashiels, attended by Sir Walter Scott as a guest of Deacon Walker, the poet entertained the company with his one and only song.

> Tarry 'Oo' Tarry 'Oo',
> Tarry 'Oo' is ill to spin,
> Card it weel, card it weel,
> Card it weel ere ye begin,
> When 'tis carded, row'd and spun,
> Then the work is haflins done;
> But when woven, drest and clean,
> It may be cleading for a Queen.

'Oo' means wool, a description which may still be used today by shepherds when referring to fleece, oo shears — wool shears — sheep shears.

Nevertheless fashion changed when there arose a demand for blue cloth in the 1770s, bringing a new trade of dyeing to the mill towns. For fifty years the blue cloth remained popular, its fall from favour in 1828 creating one of the first depressions suffered by the tweed industry and leaving manufacturers with large stocks of unwanted material. As weaving skills and machinery developed patterned clothes were woven — checks and tartans mixtures. During the ten-year period from the mid-1860s the population of Galashiels expanded from five to fifteen thousand. Business boomed for the mills towards the end of the nineteenth century, when in fact the last of the major mills was built in Gala. Many of them have now been demolished such was the boom and burst of a trade heavily dependent upon export markets.

Sir Walter Scott was responsible for setting a fashion in dress using the products of the Border Mills. The cloth itself was first known as tweed after a London Agent mistook the word 'tweel' in the handwriting of a clerk from William Watson's mills for 'tweed'. Scott's choice was for trousers in shepherd's check or plaid, worn with a plain black jacket which became known as the 'tweedie'. From here developed the suit as we know it today in that all the materials in jacket, waistcoat and trousers were 'suited' to each other.

Wars throughout Europe and the American Civil War from the 1850s onwards had been beneficial in creating an export market to embattled countries whose own manufacturing industry had been interrupted by conflict. A hammer blow was around the corner when in 1890 a tariff of 49½ per cent was imposed by the American Government on all imported woollen goods. It was known as the McKinley tariff but worse was around the corner when the import levy was raised to a crushing 57 per cent. A quarter of the Galashiels workforce lost their jobs, many emigrating to escape the spectre of poverty by Tweedside. No doubt many of the Braw Lads who went oversees were instrumental in setting up textile trades in their adopted countries.

Since then the Galashiels tweed industry's decline has continued, sometimes slowly, sometimes rapidly. European markets assisted for a time; the 1914–18 war brought increased demand while the hard times of the 1920s brought a further slump. Changes in tailoring to machine-made clothes required mass produced cheaper cloth from English mills whereas Galashiels had always aimed at the high-class quality market. By the late 1930s five of the largest mills were closed, never to re-open.

The marketing system of selling all finished cloth through merchants was a further constriction upon the Galashiels industry, as manufacturers strove to produce new designs to keep up with the trends of fashion when tweed was adopted for ladies' fashion. Even then in the years between the two world wars cloth design for clothes to clad the fair sex were at the whim of distant fashion gurus and planned production was becoming almost impossible.

Alongside Gala Water the mills, once the key to the town's prosperity, stand empty or the sites are cleared or the old buildings converted for new uses, mainly for the service industries. The railway responsible for much industrial expansion is now utilised in places as a pleasant walkway beside the river.

In fact at the Peter Anderson mill, conducted tours of the premises will reveal the methods in use for producing some of this high-quality cloth today. Here we learn that 800 years after the Flemish monks from the Border abbeys introduced the seed head of the teasel plant as a means of cloth finishing, this humble aid is still used in the final process for fine cashmere and mohair cloth. These are imported from the south of France, before around one thousand are mounted on drums between which the cloth passes to be brushed and smoothed. Amazingly no replacement has been found for this natural brush, which despite its fragile appearance, lasts for six months before requiring replacement.

Water power to drive the mills was first utilised in the late seventeenth century when two small burns were diverted into a lade, an artificial waterway, leading to the mills. As demand grew the Gala Water itself was also tapped bringing extra reusable power through the lades; for instance, the lade which drove the Peter Anderson Mill in the late nineteenth century, provided power for a further fifteen mills.

At Peter Anderson's the turbine which replaced an earlier water wheel in 1860 was capable of running the four floors of the mill for twelve to sixteen hours a day, six days a week before doing the same job in the next mill downstream. The turbine no longer drives the mill but is used for demonstration purposes during the mill tours.

Once the entire operation from washing and carding the raw fleeces took place under the one roof, water drawn from the mill lade being used in the process before being discarded back into the lade. With the use of many imported fleeces this led to an astounding 348 foreign plant species becoming established downstream, especially where the Gala Water enters the Tweed. As these fleeces arrived in bales of raw wool which had received no primary treatment, the wealth of prickly plant seeds which they held can only be imagined.

Despite the initial processes involving alkali and sulphuric acid at temperatures reaching 180 degrees, these alien plants thrived for a time to such an extent that British botanists were able to study the colonies and inform their counterparts in

South Africa, Australia and South America upon plants which were as yet unknown in their own countries. Yet for some of these plants the southern hemisphere was not their native habitat, having arrived there from Spain on the fleeces of breeding stock exported to southern climes, where both carrier and carried thrived.

Working conditions in the mills along Gala Water are said to have been better than those in contemporary weaving centres in England. Even so men, women and children over the age of eight were expected to put in a fourteen-hour six-day week at the looms. Younger children alternated between work and school and in addition to their 6p per day received a suit of clothes and a bonnet per annum. Apprenticeships lasted between five and six years, where the rules included not frequenting ale houses or keeping bad company upon the pain of a 20s (£1) fine. Employers on the other hand were obliged to give their charges a full and proper training and board and clothe the apprentice during his period of training.

At the North Wheatlands Mill, 'The Borders Wool Centre' on the Stewart and Ramsden premises shows wool from its first stage, right to the finished article. Although no commercial spinning or weaving is carried out on the premises, the buildings are still used for the grading and sorting of locally grown fleeces. The display starts at the very beginning with live exhibits of sheep in outdoor pens. In the visitor section of the mill a sample of fleeces from numerous different breeds is on hand for the visitor to experience by touch the properties of various breeds. Wool from the Cheviot breed is the mainstay of the Harris tweed cloth; the hard-wearing properties of the Blackface, on the other hand, makes it ideal for carpet weaving, while Border Leicester Cross is excellent for handknitting and Shetland for fine knitting yarns, to name but a few.

Available at The Borders Wool Centre is a wide selection of the end products from the sheep of the Border hills — knitwear, yarns, tweed cloth and even items made from horn. This latter was once a trade in its own right, making spoons and other domestic items from the only part of the sheep which could not be eaten or worn. Hand-spinning demonstrations are a regular feature during the summer months, along with regular showings of British Wool video films.

Textiles College Gala.

The esteem in which the Borders textile industry is held, is reflected in the siting of the Scottish College of Textiles at Netherdale in Galashiels. As discussed in Chapter 1, the establishment at Gala is the Faculty of Textiles of Heriot-Watt University. Students from Britain and overseas (the halls of residence cater for 200) attend the courses covering every aspect of the trade. These include management, design, colour science, clothing and marketing. Course studies lead to anything from National Certificates, through H.N.C. and H.N.D. to BSc and MSc in the chosen subjects.

As some aspects of textile manufacturing have declined, other industries have arisen, not exactly replacing the jobs lost in the old mills but bringing a new age of technological expertise to the Borders. From a room above the British Linen Bank in Galashiels High Street two local men, Robert Currie and Ken Mill, began experiments in the early 1960s with a new innovation in the dawning age of electronics, printed circuit boards. With a total capital of £500 the firm moved to Abbots Mill, bringing to Galashiels a new industry for a town too long dependent upon cloth manufacturing. Eventually Robert Currie and Ken Mill parted company, Robert going on to found

Exact Circuits, now part of the giant Standard Telephones and Cables Ltd. Ken Mill in turn set up Bepi (Electronics) Ltd. Bepi was first taken over by Pye but is now part of another giant international Philips Group, still operating in Galashiels.

The Gala Water which was so vital for the early mills, begins life high in the Moorfoots on the Lothian watershed upon the slopes of Hunt Law. After joining with the Heriot Water, Gala Water takes a twisting winding course south to meet the Tweed. Alongside runs the A7 trunk road on the east bank, although the original road follows the west. Here once ran the Waverley Line, its trackbed and bridges perhaps the most intact of all the one-time railways in the Borders.

Beside the Gala Water the Arthurian Legend lingers in the one-time name of the valley Weadale, or the dale of woe, where tradition records that King Arthur suffered a major defeat. Like all Arthur legends the true story is lost in the mist of time; what is more certain is that Stow or the Stow of Weadale, the principal village in the valley, dates from Saxon times and means stock or stockade.

Religious activity here dates from at least the seventh century when Stow was one of the three principal seats of sanctuary in Scotland and a place of special reverence. The ruins of the old parish church of Stow date from a building founded in the

Pack Horse Bridge over Gala Water at Stow.

fifteenth century with considerable alterations in the seventeenth and eighteenth. The original consecration, however, took place in 1242. Downstream of the village stands the modern church, whose clock has such a reputation for accuracy that train drivers on the line below checked their own regulation watches by it.

Opposite this church can be seen the first bridge to have been constructed over the Gala Water; prior to this crossings were by ford when water levels permitted. The bridge is described as a pack horse bridge built in 1665, the cost being raised by public collection. Much of the stone used in its unusual low parapet construction came from the choir of the old church.

Stow, one of the highest villages in the Borders, was once attached to St Andrews. Here the bishop had his summer residence when the income of the old church of Stow and the surrounding area was included among the lands of the Bishop of St Andrews. Two gables remain of the Bishop's House but excavations have revealed that this was once a much larger complex.

Returning to Galashiels, Abbotsford lies just across the Tweed, giving Scott strong links with Gala, but it was Robert Burns who penned the words paying tribute to young men of Galashiels in his poem, since set to the music of a traditional tune arranged by Haydn.

> Braw, braw lads on Yarrow braes
> Ye rove among the blooming heather;
> But Yarrow braes nor Ettrick Shaws,
> Can match the lads o' Gala Water,
> Braw, braw lads.

Perhaps Scotland's national bard was thinking about the incident in 1337 when a party of English soldiers were surprised by foresters from Galashiels, while the former were gathering 'soor plooms' (sour plums which we know as sloes). Tradition says that the 'Englishmen's Syke' ran red with blood for three days and nights. From this incident sprang the town motto, 'Sour Plums', the fruit being depicted in the Burgh Coat of Arms. A local boiled sweet, 'soor plooms', reflects the sweet tooth of other Border Towns; both soor plooms and Hawick balls are now made by a Hawick firm.

Not surprising is the local festival, 'The Braw Lads Gathering', when one of the events is a rideout to the Raid Stane at the 'Englishmen's Syke' where symbolic twigs of soor ploom are pinned to the jacket of the principal riders. The Gathering, when compared to traditional Common Riding is a fairly recent event, first established in 1930 but this in no way detracts from the enthusiasm of its followers. Even so The Gathering could be looked upon as a revival of the earlier Midsummer Fair which had been discontinued.

Principals in The Gathering are the Braw Lad and Braw Lass, who are appointed by an executive council. To both Lad and Lass are allocated two attendants or supporters, all of whom have a role to play during the celebrations. To the male attendants falls the role of bearers of the Sod and Stone from Torwoodlee, then eventually to the Market Cross. This is symbolic — the Sod representing the Forest and the Stone heritable property — simulating the act of Sasine in the gifting of Ettrick Forest by James IV to his bride Margaret Tudor.

The Braw Lad cuts the sod at Torwoodle, pronounced as Torudlee locally.

The ceremony at Torwoodlee in a clearing beside the old tower, long since replaced by a more comfortable mansion for the Pringles of Gala, is one of the original ceremonies devised for the Braw Lads Gathering. Here the Braw Lad asks permission from the laird to remove sod and stone from Torwoodlee, which is readily granted. Should you wonder how the old tower still remains standing with the removal of a stone each year, it must be pointed out that the same stone is used today as in 1930. Able assistance is given in the ceremony by the Galashiels Silver Band, playing naturally, 'The Braw Lads' and 'The Bonny Lass o Torwoodlee', before the sod and stone are borne back to the Burgh Buildings to perform their function later in the ceremony at the Old Town Cross.

Saturday's main rideout continues from the Raid Stane by Abbotsford, then the Old Town Cross where the ceremony commemorates the marriage of Margaret Tudor to James IV, leading eventually through descent to the Union of the Crowns. Red and white roses are presented to the Braw Lass by her attendants to be mingled in token of the houses of York and Lancaster and placed among thistles on the cross. Concluding the ceremony the Braw Lad advances upon the mounted reiver at the War Memorial to pay homage to those who fell in the present century's conflicts.

Galashiels and Sir Walter Scott's home at Abbotsford go hand in hand; doubtless both Melrose and Selkirk could lay equal claims due to Abbotsford's situation between where Ettrick and the Gala Water enter the Tweed. Walter Scott may not have been born a Borderer but by descent, inclination and choice he was and is without doubt regarded as one of the most famous Borderers of all time.

Scott claimed among his forefathers the illustrious figure of Auld Wat of Harden, coming down to Scott through Wat's son, allegedly forced to marry Sir Gideon Murray's daughter. A grandson from this marriage, known as Beardie as he refused to shave until a Stewart sat again upon the Scottish throne, was in turn father to Robert Scott of Sandyknowe, Walter's grand-father.

Scott's father must have decided that farming was not for him as he left Sandyknowe to enter into the law profession at Edinburgh. Scott's early Border connection with his grandfather's farm at Sandyknowe is dealt with at length in Borders 1, his appointment as Sheriff Depute for Selkirkshire and his stay at Ashistiel elsewhere in this book.

Abbotsford was formerly the farm house Cartley Hall, termed Clarty Hole by rude locals, and was purchased by Sir Walter in 1811. It was owned previously by Dr Robert Douglas of Galashiels, who was a prime mover in the development of the weaving industry in Gala. Scott's desire for the property may have been smouldering since early years. Once, when but a boy, his father had shown him a stone set in the river bank nearby marking a fray, between on the one hand the Homes, Kerrs and Earl of Angus and on the other the Scott of Buccleuch and his supporters, over the possession of young James V. It is known as Turn-Again, marking the spot where the fleeing Scotts turned upon their pursuers, when an Elliot slew Andrew Ker of Cessford with a spear thrust. Both Angus and Scott factions are said to have suffered heavy losses in this (allegedly the last) clan battle in the Borders, where Angus maintained possession of the sixteen-year-old king. The event is remembered in place names of Skirmish — corrupted into Skinners Hill, Turn-Again and Charge Law.

Scott recalls the fight in the first cant of 'The Lay of the Last Minstrel'.

> When first the Scott and Carr were foes;
> When royal James beheld the fray,
> Prize to the victor of the day;
> When Homes and Douglas in the van,
> Bore down Buccleuch's retiring clan,
> When gallant Cessford's heart-blood dear
> Reeked on dark Elliot's Border spear.

Despite the tumbledown state of Cartley Hall — the Clarty Hole jibe is said to be well justified — this was an ideal site for Scott. Were not the Eildons, cleft by Michael Scott, within near sight and the Catrail in which he had a keen interest could be seen just across the river. Then again the place was nigh to Scott's many promised lands: Selkirk, the valleys of Ettrick and Yarrow and the abbeys of Melrose and Dryburgh.

Extensions were made first to the old house, where during the earlier years of occupancy the Scott family endured ex-

Abbotsford, Sir Walter Scott's dream home.

tremely cramped conditions. The one main public room served many functions, as sitting and dining room, school room and study where Scott wrote in a curtained-off area beside the window. By 1814 he had made some outlying places into two spare bedrooms, kitchen and laundry; a 'handsome boudoir' opening into the drawing room was added two years later. Eventually in 1822 the old farmhouse was demolished and work began on the new Abbotsford. Finally in 1825 Scott was able to write that 'Abbotsford is now all that I can make it'. Further extensions to Abbotsford were made by James Hope-Scott who married Charlotte Lockhart (the only surviving grandchild?).

Open to the public from March to October, a visit to Abbotsford on a quiet summer's day when no coaches throng the car park is a worthwhile experience. With the windows flung open to allow a cooling breeze to filter through the dark wood-panelled rooms, the soft coo of the wood pigeon just reaching the ear, you could have easily stepped back a century and a half. In these circumstances it is not difficult to imagine the figure of Scott seated at his writing desk, surrounded by his favourite dogs, penning away at yet another Waverley novel as he strove to clear his personal commitment to Ballantyne, his publishers, and to his creditors.

Scott had little time to enjoy Abbotsford as in 1826 the publishing firm of Ballantyne collapsed with debts of £100,000, a massive sum in those times. There was no other way for Scott to repay this money to creditors other than by his pen. In an immense effort — some say it contributed to his death at 62 years of age — Scott cleared £90,000 of the money owed by Ballantynes in eight years, the remaining £10,000 being cleared after his death through copyright sales.

None of Scott's four children enjoyed long life, neither Charles nor Walter his sons having any issue, leaving it up to his eldest daughter Sophia and his son-in-law and later biographer J.S. Lockhart to continue the Scott blood if not name. Scott's eldest grandson by Sophia died aged ten and with the early death of his brother Walter his sister Charlotte became heir.

She in turn married James Hope, a cadet of the Earl of Hopetoun, adopting the name of Hope Scott. A daughter from this union, Mary Monica, married the son of Lord Herries, the Hon Joseph Constable-Maxwell, assuming the name of Maxwell-Scott. From this marriage the eldest son Walter received the revived baronetage in 1932, his daughters Jean and Patricia Maxwell-Scott, the great-great-great-granddaughter of Sir Walter and now custodian of the Scott name and home.

At this stage of his life on moving to Abbotsford Scott had already made a major contribution to literature and had already published three volumes of the *Minstrelsy of the Scottish Border*, a collected work of traditional ballads. His own work at this time amounted to what some consider to be his first and finest poetical work *The Lay of the Last Minstrel*, published in 1805. In 1808 *The Lay* was followed by *Marmion* and *The Life of Dryden* and two years later by *The Lady of the Lake*. Over and above his writing at the time Abbotsford was purchased, Scott had attended Edinburgh University, entering in 1783 aged 12, had met Robert Burns, was called to the Bar in Edinburgh as an advocate and had been appointed Sheriff-depute for Selkirkshire.

Of his personal life he had wooed at least once and lost. When aged 26, he married Margaret Charlotte Charpentier, the daughter of a French refugee in 1797 and their daughter Sophie was born in 1799. The young Walter Scott and his bride set up their first home at North Castle Street, Edinburgh. In the same year as Sophie was born, the Sheriff-depute of Selkirk died with the appointment of Walter Scott to the position. As Sheriff-depute Scott was required to reside for at least part of the year within the county, leading to his taking the lease of Ashiestiel, above Caddonfoot beside the Tweed, in 1804. By this time his family had increased to three children: Walter born in 1801 and Anne born in 1803; his fourth child, Charles, was born at Ashiestiel in 1805.

His appointment in 1806 as Clerk of the Court of Sessions, Scotland's supreme court, provided Scott with financial security, although this was but a drop in the ocean of the crash which followed twenty years later. July, 1814 saw the publication of *Waverley*, the first of a series which set the literary world of the time on its heels. In the early nineteenth century it did not seem fitting to one such as Scott, who held a high position in legal circles, to be acknowledged as a public entertainer writing popular novels and Scott did not claim authorship until 1827. Over a ten-year period the series grew. *Bride of the Lammermoor, Rob Roy, Heart of Midlothian* gave avid readers one of the most imposing outpourings of writing ever known.

From Abbotsford Scott was created the first baronet in George IV's reign, becoming Sir Walter in 1820. Once Abbotsford was completed, Scott began to assemble artifacts of Scottish and international historic interest. The Armoury and Entrance Hall is hung with weapons, steel bonnets and complete sets of armour. Many items were donated by his friends but Scott travelled far afield, visiting among other sites the field of Waterloo in his search for items to grace the walls of Abbotsford.

Acquired by Scott also were items relating to some of Scotland's greatest figures of the past: Rob Roy's gun, a sword belonging to Montrose, Prince Charlie's quaich, a model of the skull of Robert the Bruce, not to mention a library of over 9,000 rare books. All of these can yet be seen at Abbotsford today.

As always Scott retained an immense interest in his native land. It is said that he spoke not with the affection of the upper classes of the day. His voice rather has been described as a soft Border burr which is understandable as although he commanded the respect and friendship of all ranks of society, Scott communicated as much with the ordinary man on moor or at market. It was his love for Scotland that led to the re-discovery of the Scottish Crown and Sceptre and the Sword of State which had lurked unseen for overlong in dusty vault and chest.

By far the most impressive and famous monument to Sir Walter Scott dominates the principal street of Scotland's capital city. However it is mere stone and lime, as is Abbotsford; the best memorials to Scott lie between the covers of his novels and poetical works.

# CHAPTER 7

## *Lower Tweeddale*

Just upstream of Galashiels the Tweed assumes the aspect of an upland water; pools are now smaller streams and more frequent while in places the bare bedrock protrudes through the river bed. Tweed's name origins are somewhat obscure when compared with those of her tributaries. River names, incidentally, are considered to be one of the truest indicators of the earliest peoples in many parts of Scotland. Some scholars consider the name Tweed to be of Celtic origin meaning 'swelling, powerful or raging stream' and having been given to the Angles by native tribes; other sources say that the name is entirely Teutonic and replaced an earlier Celtic one.

Whatever is the true name source, there are few places in the lower part of Tweeddale between Gala and Peebles where the Tweed in normal flow is tumultuous and reckless. Sprightly and rippling would aptly describe the sequence of stream and pool found here. From Galashiels the A72 scorns the Tweed as it

Here near Peel, the waters of Tweed could well be described as 'rushing'.

leaves the town, following Gala Water to pass between Mains Hill and Meigle Hill past the village of Clovenfords which was once famous for the quality of grapes grown here.

Sometimes wending upstream beside the Tweed, the surrounding hills soon force road and river together. One of the narrowest parts of the Tweed valley can be found at the boundary between Ettrick and Lauderdale and Tweeddale. Upstream at the towns of Walkerburn and Innerleithen the valley opens out, where the broad haughs accommodate the milltowns which developed here in the heyday of the woollen industry. Walkerburn has one of the few caulds on the Tweed which diverted the river into lades to drive the machinery of the first mills.

Sharing the riverside, traces of the old Caledonian railway which served Peebles from Galashiels are easily detectable. In the railway boom two companies competed for freight and passenger traffic in Tweeddale, Peebles having two railway stations on the north and south banks of the Tweed. On the north bank the North British railway cut over the hills from Leadburn, while on the south the Caledonian line arrived up Tweedside. One of the most obvious of the remaining relics of the railway era can be found in the iron bridge, with its three stone piers, which now serves as a footbridge near Cardona.

Forestry clads many of the hillsides on both sides of the river — Elibank and Traquair Forests, Yair and Cardona on the south bank with Glentress Forest on the north. By Traquair the motorist can cross to Yarrow by the Paddock Slack while the Southern Upland Way, Minchmoor Road and a myriad of old tracks serve the walker and cyclist. Starting at Innerleithen on the north bank the B 709 offers a short cut to the driver into the Lothians or to the head of the Gala Water at Heriot, a road most suitable for the cyclist with easier gradients than by Gala Water and Stow. There is less evidence of old routes across the moorland here but forestry tracks lead deep into Glentress and from Glentress Scottish Border Trails specialise in mountain bike trekking or the day hire of A.T.B. bicycles on forestry and hill tracks.

Partly this is Ettrick and Lauderdale district giving way to that of Tweeddale in a devious boundary through the centre of Traquair Forest. These districts were the old counties of

Selkirkshire and Peeblesshire; the latter in the upper part of the Tweed Valley is sometimes considered not to be part of the Borders proper. Why this should be is uncertain; only a watershed away from Yarrow, the residents of Peeblesshire must be as much Borderers as any. Perhaps the minstrels of old did not find enough material for their ballads here to bring this part of the world into our modern acceptance of the Borders, yet there have been writers of a more recent date who have made their mark in lyrical works.

At Fairnilee a mile or so upstream from Ettrick and Tweed's confluence was born Alison Rutherford, later Mrs Cockburn, who wrote her version of the 'Flowers of the Forest'. This, according to Sir Walter Scott, was not penned to mark any particular event but was possibly a lament for the general depopulation of Ettrick Forest.

The mansion of Ashestiel was Sir Walter Scott's first home in the Borders to which he moved from his cottage at Lasswade where he and Charlotte had first set up home following their marriage. Several avenues seem to have been explored by Scott as to the home his duties required him to have in the Borders. These included Harden, the ancestral home of his branch of the Scott family. Eventually Scott decided upon renting Ashestiel, the property of his cousin, a General Russel, who was then serving with his regiment in India. So for the next eight years Walter Scott and his family settled into the old house above the Tweed. Some of Scott's happiest days were said to have been spent at Ashestiel, where, comfortable with his salary as Sheriff, he now began to reap the harvest of his pen and fertile imagination.

While he lived here some of his most notable works were written. *The Lady of the Lake, Marmion* and part of *The Lay of the Last Minstrel* first saw light of day at Ashestiel. Indeed Scott so loved the place that had he been able to purchase the estate, the grand mansion of Abbotsford might never have risen from the farm of Cartley Hall further downstream.

Two miles upstream stood Elibank Tower, actually designated as Castle on O.S. Sheet 73, now within Elibank and Traquair Forest where one of the most unusual betrothments of all time is alleged to have taken place. Here, as the story goes, came William Scott, a son of Auld Wat o' Harden, bent on replenish-

Elibank Tower, home of Gideon Murray and scene of the alleged forced marriage of Muckle-mou'ed Meg to young Scott of Harden.

ing the family larder from the beeves of Gideon Murray, Elibank's owner — something of a traditional trade with the Harden Scotts. William, according to the story, must have been a less crafty operator than his father in the cattle stealing (steaks), and gets himself caught in the act of rustling. Gideon Murray thinks that a bit of instant justice involving a length of rope, a convenient tree branch and young Scott of Harden might serve as a lesson — a final one for William but a deterrent to others who might seek the same road. But 'haud on', says his wife, 'let's no be ower hasty on this, think ye o' oor ill faired doughter.'

Apparently the young lady is known as Muckle-mou'ed Meg for obvious reasons and because of this generous width of smile Meg lacks an eager suitor. Just the very wench for young Harden, who received the proposal from Meg's father — marry Muckle-mou'ed Meg or hang the next morning. After taking a look at her Harden elects to hang but gets a night in Elibank's dungeon to think things over. In the cold light of dawn with the rope around his neck the situation acquires a new perspective. Is not after all Meg quite attractive? The wedding is soon arranged and the pair live happily ever after.

That day they were wedded, that night they were
bedded,
An' Juden has feasted them gaily an' free,
But aft the bridegroom has he rallied an'bladded,
What faces he made at the big hanging tree.

Fiction is stranger than fact in this instance, for as far as this
story goes William Scott of Harden and Agnes Murray of Elibank
signed a contract of marriage on 18th February, 1611. As the
contract document is said to extend to seven feet in length
signed by all concerned except Auld Wat, the marriage duly
took place on May 1st, 1611. No doubt Agnes, or Meg, was a
comely lass and young William Scott required no coercion in
the shape of a gallows tree to enter into the union.

What remains of the tower of Elibank can be seen high on
the hillside above the Tweed valley. Elibank appears to have
been at one time an L-shaped tower, now crumbling, but recent
repairs by the present owner have secured what remains. Below
lies the modern mansion where the descendants of Gideon
Murray built a more comfortable home when more peaceful
times fell upon the Borders. What the house cannot enjoy is
the commanding views up and down the Tweed valley. Even
from the base of Elibank tower, which lies in a corner of a
meadow surrounded by forestry, it is apparent that no travellers
could pass below in daylight without their passage being noted
by Elibank.

Walkerburn is one of the smallest of all the mill towns in the
Borders, drawing its water power from the Tweed instead of a
tributary stream. The village owes its very existence to Henry
Ballantyne, a textile weaver, who developed the settlement from
a few farm buildings to a thriving community and introduced
hydroelectric power for light and power in 1919.

Electricity offered many advantages over other forms of
power for the textile industry, the smooth continuous drive
being much more compatible with many of the processes than
that obtained from water or even steam. Ballantyne's hydro
scheme was years before its time; today it would be described
as a 'pumped storage system' — in 1919 it was called 'The
Mechanical Storage of Power'.

From turbines sited on the mill lade around 220 h.p. were

available, falling short by 230 h.p. for what was required to run the Tweedvale mill. A solution was found by building a reservoir 1000ft above on Kirnie Law, capable of holding 3½ million gallons of water. This took a total of 132 hours to fill or empty but used the 220 h.p. provided by the mill lade to pump water up to the reservoir during the night when the mill was idle. The water was released through turbines when the mill was working giving the additional 230 h.p. Similar schemes have since been used by, for example, the Scottish Hydro Electric Board on a much larger scale at Ben Cruachan above Loch Awe.

Sadly, large-scale textile manufacture no longer takes place at Walkerburn. The Scottish Museum of Woollen Textiles and The Mill Shop now occupy Tweedvale Mill. Here the exhibits trace the development of wool from the shearing of Cheviot sheep to the finished woven or knitted garments. Starting with a simple spindle for spinning and continuing through the different versions of the spinning wheel, the visitor sees the progress, right up to the Crompton Mule, from cottage to mill industry.

Redundant examples of buildings which once housed the woollen industry can be seen in all the mill towns of the Borders; mill owners earlier this century certainly built to last. Many are outstanding examples of industrial architecture deserving a better fate than a roost for feral pigeons. Currently Scottish Borders Enterprise are revamping the Walkerburn mills into industrial units; the first phase was formally opened by H.R.H. Prince Edward in spring 1992.

Already established here is the firm J.D.L. Engineering run by John White, a firm which develops and manufactures highly technical machinery for the printing trade. Found within the same building is the Borders' only involvement in the aviation industry, run by John's son Alistair. A keen amateur pilot himself, Alistair is agent for 'Kitfox', an American firm which produces light aircraft which, as the name suggests, arrive more or less in boxes and crates.

With a frame of light strong steel of the same specification as is used in the best quality racing bicycles, the fabric-covered Kitfox takes around some 700 hours to assemble. Returning an astonishing 30 miles per gallon depending upon the choice of engine, the Kitfox can take off in 100ft with only the pilot

Innerleithen on a broad Tweedside haugh.

aboard but requires at least a 300-yard runway for safe operation. What the Kitfox lacks in size and speed it makes up for in convenience — with wings folded the plane is easily loaded on a trailer for transporting between home and any convenient landing strip.

Innerleithen sits astride the Leithen Water just where this tributary enters the Tweed; once the Leithen was harnessed as a power source and the diverting cauld and part of the old lade can still be seen. The town sprang to prominence as a centre of weaving around 1788 when Alexander Brodie, who had served an apprenticeship as a blacksmith at nearby Traquair, built a factory to give employment to the people of his native district. Brodie had left Tweedside some thirty years earlier with the princely sum of 17s 6d in his pocket to become a leading London iron master with a fortune of half a million pounds. Today there is only one firm involved in the weaving industry in Innerleithen, but seven with varied capacities in knitwear, the emphasis being upon high-quality cashmere and garments involving a high degree of hand finishing.

If Brodie established prosperity for Innerleithen, Scott brought about its popularity with his only novel set in his own times, *St Ronans Well*, which was immediately identified as set in

Innerleithen. Published in 1823 *St Ronan's Well* brought Innerleithen into prominence as a fashionable watering place; the mineral spring known as the Doos' Well was rapidly changed to St Ronan's by the canny citizens — no doubt with their eye on a sovereign or two to be gained.

In an analysis of the water in 1882, a Dr Fyfe seems to have considered its qualities a cure for almost all ills, from 'General Debility of the System' to 'Sterility'. On the latter he considers 'In cases of sterility the Innerleithen Spa has been found of the greatest service; and married Ladies who had long given up hopes of having a family, by taking a regular course of the waters have found themselves in a state which "Ladies wish to be who love their Lords."'

Over the next two decades Innerleithen's popularity soared as a spa and fashionable watering hole, an essential place for the socially ambitious to be seen at. A pavilion was built over the site in 1827 on the orders of Charles Stuart, the eighth in his line and last Earl of Traquair. Today every supermarket sports bottles of mineral, in other words spa water. In Britain at least St Ronans Well was the first spa to provide a take-away system, with a bottling plant which still continues to this day through a local firm.

Gradually the fashion of taking the waters waned; the magical properties of St Ronan's Well may have become diluted by water from other springs. Attempts were made to revitalise the wells in the closing years of the nineteenth century by tracing their source and piping the water to a renovated pavilion. By 1966 the site was becoming neglected and was purchased at this time by the Innerleithen Town Council. A St Ronan's Well Appeal Fund has been formed by local residents with the backing of the Shell Wildlife Fund. They have created a new Interpretive Centre at St Ronan's Well where the public may yet partake of the famous waters.

St Ronan's Wells plays an important part in Innerleithen's local festival, not based upon riding the bounds or celebrating battles but dedicated to ridding the district of the devil. This duty was said to have been undertaken by St Ronan away back in the eighth century, hence the sulphurous nature of the Wells where the saint is said to have cleiked the De'il.

Devised by a Galashiels man in 1900 the Cleikum

St Ronan's Well, Innerleithen.

Ceremony's principal performer is the Dux boy of the local school who represents St Ronan in the ceremony, supported by saintly classmates and an elected adult Standard Bearer. The Cleikum Ceremony compliments St Ronan's Games, founded in 1827. The event has been patronised by some of the greatest literary figures of the day — Scott and Professor Wilson or Christopher North as he was known. James Hogg seems to have played a prominent part in the event, acting not only as patron but as competitor and after-dinner entertainer also.

Within Robert Smail's Printing Works on Innerleithen High Street can be found a business unchanged for over a hundred years. Now a National Trust property, run partly as a museum, the works still undertake commercial printing using techniques and machinery virtually unchanged since their installation when Queen Victoria ruled over half the globe.

Print is still set by hand. Visitors may have a try, but mind your 'Ps' and 'Qs', letters instantly identified in capitals but easily jumbled in lower case. At Robert Smail's the visitor learns that once a seven-year apprenticeship was required for this labour-intensive task. The firm was at one time both a newspaper printer and publisher. The compositor's or 'comps' skill was in laying out the page to be pleasing to the eye and where possible eliminating 'widows' and 'orphans'. Locked into flat metal frames the completed work went downstairs to the machine room where the most modern printing press is fifty years old. Other machines date from times when 'Armstrong's patent' was the moving force which transferred the message on the inked type to paper, prior to the introduction of water power to drive the presses.

Robert Smail's is an amazing place especially in that the proprietor almost never flung anything away; consequently a record is retained of every job undertaken by the firm. Here lies another story, as after a lifetime of magpie instincts, Robert Smail decided that he should clear the contents of the office on the morning upon which the National Trust was taking over the building, so the Trust's officer had to rescue boxes of records from the very jaws of the refuse crusher.

Although for centuries nearby Traquair was the more important settlement, Innerleithen does have an ancient history, the church here having been granted to the monks of Kelso around 1159 by Malcolm IV. Rights of sanctuary were accorded to the church as this was said to be the first resting place of the body of one of Malcolm's sons who was drowned on a hunting expedition in a deep, dark, Tweed pool, long known as Droonpooch. It is said that Innerleithen was anciently known as Hornehuntersland, so the town could well have ancient royal connections.

As Innerleithen grew so Traquair village declined, until today the latter is a mere hamlet adjacent to Traquair House, which itself is reputed to be the oldest building in Scotland in continuous habitation. Throughout the Borders can be found mansion houses designed by the most prestigious architects of the day to impress and emphasise their owner's importance and social standing, yet Traquair which just grew from a square keep seems the more attractive by its sheer simplicity. Traquair House sports no ornate balustrades, no imitation battlements nor does it flaunt architectural features from around Europe. Thick rubble-built walls, small windows and steeply pitched rooflines do not indicate the pen of some great architect. Rather the style is local, practical and functional for wind-and watertightness.

Traquair House, oldest inhabited dwelling in Scotland, scaffolded for repairs in summer 1992.

But think on when you visit Traquair, as visit you surely must; as you squeeze up the narrow stairs in the oldest part of the building, here you follow in the footsteps of a Scottish monarch of 1000 years ago.

Exactly when the first building was erected at Traquair is uncertain, but it was possibly a royal residence in the shape of a Royal Hunting Lodge in the reigns of David I to Alexander III, beginning in the early part of the twelfth century. The first documented evidence of Traquair is from the reign of Alexander, dated 1107. Ownership changed: Lord James Douglas was one, followed by Murrays, Boyds, William Rogers (James III's unfortunate favourite who met a dire fate at Lauder, as described in '*Discovering the Borders 1*') through to the present-day Stuarts.

Not surprisingly the old house has seen its share of famous

and notorious visitors over the passage of time. Mary Queen of Scots with her then husband Lord Darnley was among the twenty-seven regal bodies who have found shelter within the ancient walls; the oak cradle which rocked the infant James VI is only one of many historic artifacts retained at Traquair. The most recent visit by a reigning monarch was in 12th July, 1923 by George V and Queen Mary, accompanied by the Duke and Duchess of York, who after the abdication of the Duke's brother became George VI and Queen Elizabeth, the present Queen Mother.

The first Earl of Traquair was for a time Lord High Treasurer of Scotland, about the highest post in the land in the early seventeen century, from which he later fell to spend his last days begging in the streets of Edinburgh before dying in a cobbler's house. Prior to his decline the Earl had been involved in a lawsuit, the outcome of which was to be decided in the Court of Session under the presidency of the incorruptible Lord Durie who held the casting vote.

As the final verdict was predicted to be a close run thing with the result likely to hang on Lord Durie's decision (and he was known to be unsympathetic to Traquair), it seemed in true Border fashion that the best course of action would be to remove Durie until the matter was settled. Here Traquair enlisted the help of one William Armstrong, Christie's Will, whose forebearer had been so rudely dealt with by James V at Carlanrig in Teviotdale. Christie's Will's release from Jedburgh Tollbooth had been solicited by Traquair; apparently Will faced the same fate as his illustrious ancestor — his crime the theft of two bridles which still had horses attached.

Anyway the time had come for Will to return the favour bestowed on him by Traquair; perhaps a century earlier it would have been a simple throat-cutting job, but after the Union of the Crowns these were more civilised times. From Leith Sands, where Lord Durie is known to frequently walk, Christie's Will abducts him, carrying the lord off to a gloomy tower in Annandale (although in Scott's ballad Durie is lured away rather than kidnapped). He is held here for three months, well-cared for but with no human communication, until the lawsuit is settled in Traquair's favour. Traquair then sends Christie's Will the message:

'Ye may let the auld brock oot the poke;
The land's my ain, and a's gane weel.'

That then is one Traquair tale although the best known is that of the Bear Gates, the 'Steekit Yetts', which tradition says were closed behind the Bonnie Prince, never to be re-opened until another Stuart sat on the Scottish Throne. Despite being staunch Jacobites and Catholics, for some reason the Stuarts did not support the '45 uprising. Charles Edward Stuart had ridden from Edinburgh or Kelso in person to persuade Traquair to come out; however as the Bear Gates closed behind Prince Charlie the laird vowed that so they would remain until once again a Stuart was king of Scotland.

Other often quoted versions of the closing of the Bear Gates include that of the 7th earl shutting them behind the cortege bearing his young wife away from Traquair, but are incorrect. Again the story is that they would never re-open until another countess sat in Traquair, but as the lady in question had died in Spain, no credence is given to this story by the Stuart family.

Not surprisingly the oldest inhabited house in Scotland is open to the public at Easter, then from May to September, while the Traquair Fair is an annual event held within the grounds. Not all is show, however, as practical work still goes on in the ancillary buildings around the house which have been adapted as craft workshops including woodturning, printing and pottery. Within the grounds where peacocks strut and semi-tame chaffinches share your picnic lunch, can be found walks beside the Quair Water, a maze and some splendid woodland of mature trees.

Houses great and small throughout the Borders — in fact throughout Scotland — would at one time have brewed their own ale for domestic consumption. Before tea and coffee became common cheap beverages ale was the drink taken with most meals. Since 1965 the practice of brewing has been resurrected at Traquair, using original equipment which had lain unused for over two hundred years when the imposition of a malt tax made small-scale brewing uneconomic. Gas now fires the brewing vat instead of coal, but otherwise the wooden fermentation vessels and cooling trays remain, having withstood the ravages of time and the years of disuse.

Bear Gates, Traquair, locked behind the Bonnie Prince until a Stuart once more reigns in Scotland.

Traquair Ales are traditional or real ales, brewed to a recipe dating from the 1600s, although earlier versions date from the 1300s. Some of these no doubt were drunk by Mary Queen of Scots on her visit. Only natural ingredients are used in the brew — malted barley, hops and water from Traquair's own spring.

Two standard brews are produced: Traquair House Ale at 7.2. per cent and Bear Ale Draught at 5 per cent. On special occasions, such as the celebration of the Stuarts 500 years at Traquair in 1991, a special brew is produced and Fair Ale for the annual Traquair Fair. A small brewery such as Traquair is incapable of producing large quantities of beer; the very process of fermentation itself cannot be hurried when producing a traditional ale. Much of the production is sold before brewer Ian Cameron tips the first barrel of malt to steep; in fact a three-month waiting list exists but fear not, Traquair Ale can be bought at the house shop, while it is also available on draught in one Peebles Hotel and two discerning Edinburgh establishments.

Before setting out for Peebles, Tweed's south bank is well worth following to visit Kailzie Gardens, where a mixture of woodland and waterside gardens and a display of waterfowl can be found among the seventeen acres of pleasure gardens.

Peebles, once the centre of administration for Peeblesshire, serves the same role today for the Tweeddale District with headquarters at Rosetta Road. Sitting astride the Eddleston Water, or as it is known locally, 'the Cuddy', the name Peebles itself is said to be based upon an early Welsh word 'Pebyll', meaning tent.

Holding a long association with the kings of Scotland dating back to before the Stuart dynasty, it is possible that Peebles was a Royal Burgh in the reign of David I, although there is no existing charter to confirm this. Tweeddale District Council, successor to the Royal and Ancient Burgh, is unique in the Borders in having available a stretch of 'Town Water' available for salmon fishing through Royal Charter. Also administered by the Council is a beat from Neidpath to Hay Park leased from the Crown.

Losing burgh status was cause for lament among Gutterbluids, as native-born Peebleans are known, as opposed to those who are discovering the town who are called Stooryfits, i.e., dusty-footed incomers. Stooryfit may have had a derogatory meaning once upon a time, but today more than any other Border town Peebles has geared itself up for tourism. It is difficult to analyse why Peebles is such a popular destination for the tourist; David I did not build one of his abbeys here on the Tweed's banks. Perhaps it is simply the clean pleasant appearance of the town, its broad High Street, riverside walks and the presence in and around the town of many historical sites. Accommodation ranges from the famous Peebles Hydro

Hotel, the largest in the Borders, through smaller hotels, bed-and-breakfast establishments to two excellent camping and caravan sites.

Peebles' Mercat Cross, bearing the arms of the Burgh and the Frasers of Neidpath, has had quite a chequered history. Dating from before 1320 the Cross stands today at Eastgate on the approach to Peebles from Gala. Originally its site was in the Old Town, in what is now Young Street; from here it moved to Eastgate, was demolished in 1807 but the main parts preserved to be set up behind the Chambers Institution in 1859. Transferred to the High Street in 1895 the demands of modern traffic brought it to its present position in 1965.

James I is accredited with the poem 'Peebles to the Play' and the frolics of the Beltane Fair.

> At Beltane, when ilk body bounds
> To Peblis to the Play,
> To hear the singing and the sounds
> Their solace sooth to say;
> By firth and forest forth they found,
> They graythit them full gay;
> God wait that wald they do that stound,
> For it was their Feast day,
> They said,
> Of Peblis to the Play.

Although the Beltane Week date does not correspond with the old Beltane Festival, it does have a historical link with an ancient Celtic celebration of the sun god Baal. Beltane Week links this with the old Common Riding custom revived in 1897 to mark Queen Victoria's Diamond Jubilee — Beltane is still sometimes referred to as the Jube. Riding the Peebles Marches is documented at least as early as 1562 and doubtless the burgh boundaries had been inspected long before this time. The modern event is, of course, purely ceremonial.

Over the years Beltane week has received added attractions for Peebleans and visitors alike. The emphasis on children began in 1899 when for the first time there was a Beltane Queen supported by a First Courtier and at the same time came the first of the Crowning Ladies of the Beltane Queen. By 1924 the Cornet had a Lass, adding an official female presence to the proceedings. Honorary Wardens of Neidpath were introduced in 1929; this honour is sometimes granted to Stooryfits, including John Buchan as Lord Tweedsmuir and Sir David Steel M.P., and with some generosity it has been granted to provosts and bailies of other Border burghs. Wardens of the Cross Kirk were first elected in 1930, the post always going to ministers or priests.

It is the Beltane Queen and her court who provide the most colourful event of the Beltane week. Over five hundred children take part in the Children's Procession behind the Queen, her Maids and Courtiers, portraying an imaginative and varied assortment of characters ranging from Robin Hood and his men in the Greenwood and Snow White down to the Little Mice.

Beltane Week's highlight takes place on the nearest Saturday to mid-summer's day. The first of the proceedings begin at the early hour of 7.00a.m. when the decorated houses are judged. By 8.30 the mounted procession led by the Cornet are away by Cademuir; 9.10 sees the start of the Children's Procession, which is not a fancy dress parade, Peebles Silver Band leading the way. The day continues with proclamations, the crowning ceremony and the Grand Procession, with Cornet, Beltane Queen and Court and innumerable silver and pipe bands, through the streets of Peebles. Official finishing time is 7.00p.m. following the Beating of Retreat by the assembled bands in the High Street; in between, of course, there has been Highland Dancing and Professional Sports in Hay Lodge Park. Quite a day!

Earlier in the week one of the destinations for the Cornet's cavalcade has been Neidpath Castle, set high on a heugh overlooking the Tweed, a little upstream from Peebles. Where medieval defences are concerned Neidpath is not only the sole survivor of several peels and castles around Peebles, but also one of the best preserved castles open to the public in the Borders. This rocky eminence where the hillsides press tight against the Tweed, may have been fortified by the end of the twelfth century. The building we see there today has been the subject of much alteration, addition and deletion over the years including a siege by Cromwell's men in 1650. It was owned by the Frasers, a powerful family of feudal barons who hailed from Oliver Castle in upper Tweeddale and had arrived at Neidpath by the time of the Scottish Wars of Independence. Some errors in what was thought to be the Fraser lineage have been discovered in recent research, which is subject to copyright, but the new family tree is on view in the entrance hall at the castle. Sir Simon Fraser was one of the most notable of the line and the last Fraser to live at Neidpath. After fighting for Edward I of England at home and abroad, Sir Simon Fraser, as did Robert the Bruce, changed sides and fought against The Hammer of the Scots. Eventually he was captured and dragged to London, where like the other patriot, Wallace, he was cruelly done to death at London after a mockery of a trial in 1306.

Neidpath passed through marriage to the Hays of Yester who were lords of Tweeddale in 1686, the third earl selling the estate to the Duke of Queensbury of Douglas descent. From here it passed eventually to one known as 'old Q'; it would appear that for feats of drunkenness, debauchery and womanising few can ever claim to be his equal, although many of the tales may be grossly exaggerated as 'old Q' left quite a fortune behind.

It was 'old Q', fourth Duke of Queensbury who cleared his estates around Peebles and at Drumlanrig in Dumfriesshire of all mature timber, leaving the Tweed banks bare and desolate. This met with the disapproval of poets of the time; Burns condemned the havoc at Drumlanrig while Wordsworth put pen to paper to describe what he encountered at Neidpath. It may have been that 'old Q' wrought such havoc on the Tweedside braes to spite his heirs and successors, or perhaps to finance his wicked lifestyle. He died aged 85, hard at it right to the end. His remains lie below the Communion table in the Parish Church of St James, Piccadilly. Once again mature timber clothes the braes sweeping down to the Tweed, the deprivations of 'old Q' now but a memory.

Later in 1810 ownership passed to the Earls of Wemyss and March who are the current owners engaged in an ongoing programme of keeping the ravages of time and weather at bay. Open to the public during the summer season, Neidpath, although containing nothing in the way of furnishings or great works of art, is well worth a visit on several counts. The entrance door through the ten-foot thick walls is in fact fairly modern, the original having been over the steep bank above the Tweed making for a strong position of defence. Within the hall are a

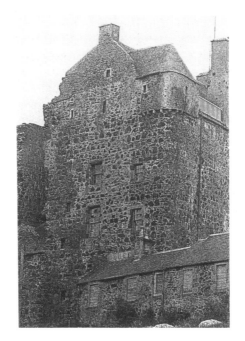

Neidpath Castle.

number of glass cases containing artifacts and information on the history of the castle and its owners.

There are cannonballs from the Cromwellian siege when it took a month of battering before the garrison surrendered and there is also an explanation of the ballistics of these early cannon and calverin which had an astonishing range and used an amazing amount of gunpowder to propel the 19–23-pound cannonball. 'Cuttings' from the Peebles 'press of yesteryear' describe the execution of wrongdoers in Peebles centuries ago, the rope to bind the sheep thief before drowning in a deep pool, the hangman's fee, loads of peat and coal to burn three witches, again the binding rope and the provision of food and drink for the dignitaries.

Downstairs from Neidpath's entrance hall is the pit prison, once only entered through a trapdoor in the floor above, but even today when lit by electricity a grim and eerie place. Beside

Rear view of Chambers Institute Peebles.

what was once the main door the porter or guard's lodge can still be seen. Upstairs the main hall and its adjacent private chamber have fireplaces, which when in use must have required a man and a boy working full time to cut and carry wood for fuel.

Recently part of the false ceiling in what is known as the Queen's Room — yet another place where Mary Queen of Scots laid her head — has collapsed, revealing the medieval ceiling hidden for centuries. In the attics the bare bones of Neidpath are revealed; the rough unhewn timber, some of it still 'in the round', has supported the castle roof for centuries.

Of course do not miss the balcony, where in times of trouble Neidpath's beacon burned, smoke by day, flame by night, to warn of approaching enemies. No hostile foe can be seen from the balcony today, but the views are superb — the Tweed directly below, then the eye wandering east over the Royal and Ancient Burgh, then down through the Tweed Valley.

What was the town house of the Dukes of Queensbury in Peebles, including the birthplace of 'old Q', forms one of the most impressive buildings on Peebles High Street. Finished in white harling in traditional local style, the building — known as the Chambers Institute — was renovated and gifted to the town by William Chambers. Natives of Peebles, William and his brother Robert founded the famous high-class publishing firm of Chambers in Edinburgh. The Peebles Institute was presented to the good folk of Peebles in 1859, not for their entertainment or amusement but for their 'social, moral and intellectual improvement'.

Prior to Peebles loosing its burgh status The Chambers Institute housed the burgh chambers for Peebles Town Council. Today after passing through the stone arch from the High Street, access is gained to the local Museum and Art Gallery run by the Tweeddale District Council. Within the museum area a varied series of exhibitions and displays is held throughout the year; sometimes the themes are local, at others they are of a general nature. That of summer 1992, for example, traced the history of Peebles from earliest times, from the hide tents of the hunter fishermen right up to the present century.

Like other Tweedside towns Peebles experienced the boom of the woollen trade in the late nineteenth and early part of the twentieth century. Gone today are the riverside mills but the weaving trade continues at March Street where Robert Noble Ltd is situated, an amalgamation of nine Border family weaving firms, who have been 'Weavers of the finest Scottish cloth since 1666'.

Lurking within the Chambers Institution behind the locked doors of what had been a library store since 1950, the glories of the 'Secret Room' were again made available to the public following a re-opening ceremony by Sir David Steel in April, 1990. Adorning the walls are plasterwork friezes cast from famous classical sculptures — namely the Alexander Frieze and the Parthenon Frieze. These copies are the work of Danish sculptor Bertel Thorvaldsen who spent some 40 years in Rome and whose work can be seen worldwide today. It is probable that the friezes were commissioned by William Chambers, no doubt aimed at the intellectual improvement of the people of Peebles.

West from the Chambers Institute can be found 'The Cornice Museum of Ornamental Plasterwork'. Within what is still a working environment can be found the moulds, or masters as they are called, for forming the ornate decoration found in many great houses throughout the Borders. Cornices, the moulding where the wall meets the ceiling, are still 'run' here, and with wellies and apron provided visitors can have a go at this craft themselves.

William Chambers is buried in the shadow of St Andrews Tower, the only remnant of the old church of St Andrews founded in 1195. The Tower in fact was restored, some say badly, by William Chambers as a memorial to himself. Destroyed by the English in 1549, assault upon the building went on over the centuries right up to Cromwellian times when Roundheads used the church as a base and stable while assaulting nearby Neidpath Castle.

Where trouble with the English was concerned Peebles was very much a Border town despite being four valleys distant from the boundary. As was the case in 1560 when the parishioners petitioned for the Parish Church of St Andrews to be replaced by the Cross Kirk as St Andrews had been 'Brint and distroyit be Yngland XII yeris syne or thairby'. Digressing from this theme for a moment: among the slain at Flodden was Patrick Gillis the burgh treasurer while the entry in burgh records of 'Brynt be our auld inimes of Yngland' is all too frequent according at least to George Burnett in his *Companion to Tweed*.

The now ruinous Cross Kirk was built by Alexander III on the advice of the Bishop of Glasgow following the discovery of a 'Stately and venerable cross' on the site. It was strongly believed at the time that the cross was in fact 'ane pairt of the verray croce thjat our Salvatour was crucifyct on'. Alongside was a stone urn containing mutilated human remains equally strongly believed to be the relics of St Nicholas.

Writing in the 1380s, over a hundred years after the discovery of the cross in 1261, 'in the presence of good men, priests, clerics and burgesses', the chronicler, John of Fordun, considers that the cross had been 'hidden by some of the faithful about the year of our Lord 296 while Maximian's persecution was raging in Britain'. A part of the shrine of St Nicholas was unearthed at the Cross Kirk earlier this century, its inscription and decorative carving remarkably intact.

Until 1784 the Cross Kirk served as a place of public worship when it was replaced by a new parish church on Castlehill. Its successor still stands there and was built in 1887 with ornate tower and crow stepped gables. No one knows what kind of castle stood on Castlehill; it may have merely been a camp of some description or a simple fort with a defensive ditch. Peebles Town Walk takes in many of these features, assisted by a booklet from the Tourist Information Office in the Chambers Institute. Few towns can boast as many Tweedside walks as Peebles, from a mere stroll in formal parks, or upstream to Neidpath with a choice in some instances of using either river bank (on the south side the rail trackbed makes for easy walking).

Unfortunately most of us, unlike John Buchan, are unable to spare the time to explore Upper Tweeddale on foot. There is much to see and many miles to cover if we are to discover this peaceful corner of the Borders; therefore it must be a combination of car and Shank's pony and a further chapter if full justice is to be done.

# CHAPTER 8

## Upper Tweedale

Peebles is the largest centre of population in Tweeddale; upstream lie only the farms and villages clustered around their kirk, a clutch of houses which today lack the convenience of village shop or post office. Despite the hills pressing ever closer the valley is fertile and productive along the riverside haughs with trig farms where the flat valley land is given over to cereals, or more likely grass growing for hay and silage and rougher grazing in the lower hills which supports suckler herds; the hill tops reaching back into the tributaries are the domain of the blackface sheep. It is not until upstream of Tweedsmuir that the uplands encroach upon the river, the lower mixture of arable and grazing now replaced by rough pasture right to the riverside. For a section the scene is entirely changed where the Badlieu forest encroaches upon the infant stream.

Upstream of Peebles the Tweed still receives some major tributaries; the first on the south bank, the Manor Water,

St Gordian's Cross in Manor Valley

reaches south deep into the hills. Manor Valley is a surprise, broad and level, so level that at Cademuir one could well imagine this to be a lake bed, which in the distant past it was. St Gordian's Cross, below Pykestone Hill, is said to have associations with a fourth-century saint of the Roman church. Of the later church which served the people of the valley nothing remains above ground level; a sandstone cross base is no doubt ancient, while an inscribed stone is dedicated to the memory of Burnetts of Barns. A more recent granite cross is dedicated 'To the dead in Christ, who sleep in God's acre, St Gordian's Kirk in peace'.

Traces of a building can be seen near the cross. A few hundred yards uphill in the shadow of a rowan tree a cement slab records that the inscribed sandstone nearby is a replica of one found here in 1890. The stone was in fact an early Christian memorial stone, which like the remains of the Peebles Cross Kirk shrine was on display at a 1992 exhibition within the Chambers Institute at Peebles.

Manor Valley was the home of Scott's real life character Davy Ritchie upon whom he based his character the Black Dwarf, in the novel of the same name. It was to the Manor Valley, to the farm of Woodhouse to be precise, that Davy Ritchie dragged his twisted misshapen body from Edinburgh where he had been apprenticed as a brushmaker. Tired of the taunts about his appearance, Davy sought solace in the solitude of Manor, near where he had been born at Easter Happrew in 1740. Davy had arrived and built his hut of large stones and turfs without the permission of the landlord, Sir James Nasmyth. Apparently he was tolerated, as later a proper house was built to replace his early crude cabin where he spent his days supporting himself, and in later years his sister, from the produce of his garden and beehives.

Scott met David Ritchie in 1797 when on a visit to Dr Adam Fergusson, a philosopher and historian who lived at the Mansion of Halyards on Manor, describing him in his introduction to *The Black Dwarf* as a poor, unhappy man. The meeting with David Ritchie is said to have flung even the redoubtable Walter Scott into a state of near shock. His novel *The Black Dwarf* was not published until 1816 some five years after the death of Davy Ritchie.

Despite his appalling deformity Davie Ritchie held himself in high esteem on some matters and picked a place for his grave in a remote spot in the glen, not wishing that 'his mortal remains would mix with the common rubbish in the kirkyard'. Later he changed his mind and poor Davy Ritchie's last resting place can be seen in the burial ground of Manor parish. To fend off the attentions of evil spirits a rowan tree was planted at Davy's grave; felled accidentally by workmen tidying up the kirkyard it is pleasing to report that a new sapling has been planted while the old stump is sending up a myriad of new growth — the Black Dwarf can well rest in peace.

The cottage can be seen today just beyond Woodside farm adjoining a sheepfold or bughts. Photographs give the impression that the building faces towards the Manor Valley road which it does not. Davy Ritchie's humble dwelling looks towards Cademuir Hill with its crown of ancient forts and settlements. Cademuir has associations with the Tweeddale Arthurian legend (more of which later) and is a steep climb. The fort remains but a ruckle of stones; the view however is superb for those who have the wind and legs to tackle the steep slope.

Macbeth's Castle, which has no known association with Macbeth King of Scots, is skirted by the unclassified road up Manor, while the remains of some of the ten-plus peels and towers which once dotted the valley can be seen on several sites. Manor Valley witnessed many events in Border history: the Thieves Road runs by Pykestone and Dollar Law to St Mary's Loch; Posso Crags on Pykestone were, in passing, famed for the quality of the falcons found in the royal eyrie there in the reign of the later James Stuart.

Eventually the motor road in Manor comes to an end, but the walker will find that it is a short distance to St Mary's Loch, while the motorist needs to make a considerable detour to reach the same destination.

Like the Manor Valley on the south side, a considerable area of Tweeddale District lies away from the valley of the Tweed. Eddleston Water leads away north through the Black Barony to Leadburn, a route shared by the main road to Edinburgh and once by the railway, and approachable also by a minor road from the A72 by the Meldon Burn, which passes between the rounded twin hills, the Black and White Meldons. Both hills are

The Meldons plaque.

crowned by forts, that on the most eastern hill, the White Meldon, being the larger of the two. Alongside the road in co-operation with local landlords several picnic areas are provided by the District Council. Plaques at these sites explain the archaeological features of the Meldons which cover the period from the Bronze Age around 2000 B.C. until the Roman occupation in 50 A.D.

As is the case in many hill forts the best aspect of the Meldons is gained from an aerial photograph, because these structures follow the natural contours of the hill tops and getting all the remains in perspective is sometimes difficult on the ground. Despite this, if sound of wind and wearing reasonable footwear the path to the top of the White Meldon is no sore trial and the views into upper Tweeddale and across to the Manor Valley are just reward for the effort. The Settlement on the lower slopes near the car park, however, once contained six huts and can be easily traced from a single standpoint and furthermore is even more easily reached than the hill fort.

A peninsula of the Borders Region occupies the north of the Tweed valley, split by the Lyne Water which rises on the flanks of the Pentlands but more or less includes all of the Tweed watershed. Tarth Water in the Borders Region, for instance, feeds by way of Lyne Water into the Tweed and nearby the Garvald Burn forms part of the boundary between the Borders and Lothian Regions but its waters are destined eventually for the Clyde.

Some of the smaller water reservoirs which supply the Lothians and Edinburgh are found above the Eddleston Lyne Waters. Portmore Loch, despite its moorland situation, is one of the most fertile in the Region where the abundance of food ensures that the stocked rainbow and brown trout here wax fat.

At West Water reservoir low water levels during the summer of 1992 revealed an important bronze-age cemetery. Considered to be at least 4000 years old, the site was brought to the notice of archaeologists by reservoir worker Andrew Moffat who spotted shards of pottery in a stone cist. Excavations on the site, which is rated as being of national importance, were carried out by the National Museum of Scotland assisted by the Lanark and District Archaeological Society and revealed a total of seven burials.

Carlops village, which lies hard against the Pentlands, was a one-time centre for the hand-loom weaving industry. West

West Linton Kirk.

Linton is, however, the largest settlement with its trim white kirk, somewhat famed for its intricate wood carvings. Quaint with narrow wynds, West Linton has a pleasant riverside park and a rather impressive children's playground opposite the kirk.

Romanno Bridge was a one-time toll place for cattle drovers taking herds south to the English markets, while in the more distant past early farmers established cultivation terraces overlooking the Lyne. An application by a building firm to construct 1000 houses on a 115-acre site at Romanno Bridge which would have increased the local population by five fold met with a 90 per cent 'no' from residents of the village who completed a questionnaire on the plans.

Another construction project, started but never finished, can be found in the ruins of Drochil Castle which is in a rather crumbling condition after the effect of three hundred years of wind and weather on the uncompleted structure. Built on the orders of James Douglas, fourth Earl of Morton and one-time regent of Scotland during the early years of James VI's rule, it

Drochill Castle.

obviously does not share the antiquity of other Border towers having been built in an era when the necessity for a defensive home had decreased.

Morton became regent in November 1572 following the death of the earl of Mar. He was sometimes described as too peace loving for his time; his two predecessors, the earls of Lennox and Moray, had both met violent deaths by shooting. Described as a loyal and capable servant of young king James, Morton was not without his faults, one being his love of money which his position allowed him to exploit in the appointment of bishops, paying the incumbent only a paltry sum and pocketing the revenues of the see himself.

With the aid of Elizabeth of England Morton recaptured Edinburgh Castle from the supporters of the young king's mother, Mary Queen of Scots, but despite this and his loyalty, Morton's brash manner did not endear him to the timid, nervous James. During his rule as regent James Douglas had improved relations with England, with an eye on James succeeding to the English throne. At the same time he is said to have done some good for the ordinary people of the land, weakening the influence of the nobles, an act which earned him numerous enemies.

It was the king's cousin, Esme Stuart, brought up in France, whose manners and attitude so suited the heir to the Scottish throne and who brought about Morton's execution. Having been created earl of Lennox, Esme would be regent, but for Morton being in the way. Bribing one James Stuart to make the accusation that Morton had prior knowledge of the murder of Darnley which he had concealed, was a fairly handy charge at the time for getting rid of unwanted nobles. Found guilty, Morton suffered an ironic fate, being the first person to be executed by the Maiden, an early form of guillotine introduced to Scotland on his behest and perhaps intended to deal with some of his opponents.

Where the Lyne takes a horseshoe bend the Romans established their major camp in Tweeddale. Most easily reached from Lyne Kirk, the squared corners of the Roman establishment are in contrast to contemporary British sites which follow the natural contours of the land. Lyne Kirk dates from the seventeenth century and has been subject to recent renovations. Part of the original roofing is preserved inside the kirk where the oaken dowels which held the original slates in place for three hundred years can yet be seen.

Working our way upriver, Stobo is the next settlement encountered along the way. Stobo Castle was built for Sir James Montgomery in baronial style in 1811. A listed building, Stobo Castle along with its unique water gardens, has been restored by the present owners as a health and beauty centre, whose clientele include some of the leading international figures in the entertainment world.

Stobo Kirk has a much older pedigree than the castle; the building as it stands is considered to be one of the oldest churches in Scotland, parts of which date from the twelfth century. The site is thought also to be that of an even earlier sixth century building founded by St Kentigern, or St Mungo as he was also known. Stobo was, in the opinion of Rev. W.S. Crockett who wrote extensively on the Borders, to be the mother church for many of the other parishes lying in the valley of the Tweed. From this tiny centre the spark of Christianity was kindled in the Tweed valley, centuries before David I founded his famous abbeys.

Stobo Kirk, an early seat of the Christian religion in Tweeddale.

While with its barrel vaulting the North Aisle would appear to be the oldest part of Stobo Kirk, it is in fact a reconstruction undertaken in 1929. Considered at the time to be the original sixth-century cell of St Kentigern, it is now thought that rather this was a mortuary aisle of fifteenth-century vintage. Incorporated in the rebuilding are several burial slabs including one of an armoured knight with massive two-handed sword.

The porch itself is a sixteenth-century addition to the nave, its walls, scored and grooved, perhaps by local archers sharpening their arrows and the damage added to by school children in later years performing the same duty with their slate pencils. Look out also for the set of jougs — a device used by the Kirk Session in administering civil punishment in the early 1700s.

A remarkable collection of trees and plants can be found at Dawyck Botanical Gardens near Stobo, now part of the Royal Botanic Garden, Edinburgh. Tree planting first began at Dawyck in 1680 when the Vietch family planted European silver firs. Over the centuries the collection has grown, much of the early collecting being done by the Nasmyth family who took over the estate in 1691. Ownership by the family continued for

Dawyck Gardens.

over two hundred years when the family sponsored many plant-collecting expeditions including those undertaken by David Douglas, who among other things, gave us the Douglas fir from the west coast of America. Trees raised from seed sent home by Douglas still grow in the Scrape Glen at Dawyck, the largest now exceeding 150 ft in height.

Eventually in 1897 the estate was purchased by Mrs Alexander Balfour; her son, employed on the west coast of North America, was instrumental in sending home more specimens of shrubs and trees which form the splendid collection today. Earlier this century the many rhododendrons were planted to give low level cover and colour and Col Balfour gifted the Arboretum to the nation in 1979. Walks at Dawyck extend uphill beside the Scrape Burn where every tree it seems has its nameplate, giving its common name where applicable, its Latin name and country of origin. Surrounded by wild cherry trees Dawyck chapel occupies the site of the old Parish Kirk, its doors now locked for the first time in 150 years due to vandalism.

Throughout the Borders flit the tales of Merlin and Arthur, a legend familiar to most people and certainly not exclusive to south-east Scotland. Unfortunately the stories of Arthur and Merlin have been embroidered over the years, detracting from the story recorded in early Welsh (Celtic) documents of Arthur the leader in the battle of the native Britons during their struggles with the Anglo-Saxon invaders around the fifth century AD, following the departure of the Romans from Britain.

Popular writing on the story of Arthur began sometime in the twelfth century, encouraged by the Plantagenet kings of England, who wished to appear as direct successors to the Arthur of the legend. The story evolved into the familiar one of a royal leader, his knights and round table. So the elaboration continued into the fifteenth century when William Caxton printed Thomas Malory's *Morte d'Arthur*; later writers and the film industry have further eroded in our minds the true story of Arthur, be he king or general.

Present-day thinking considers Arthur to be not a king, but a battle leader of Britons who may have been converted to Christianity, fighting against Anglo-Saxon invaders, among whom the Christian religion had not yet been accepted. But the legend may be even older dating back to the days before Christianity and into Celtic mythology. Many places in Britain claim to be the scene of battles fought by Arthur and his cavalry; so too can upper Tweeddale, where the possible site of the seventh battle — there are considered to have been ten — may be found on either Drumelzier Haugh, nearby Lyne, or upon the hill forts of Cademuir or Lour.

Mythology and legend place some of Arthur's battles in the wood of Caledon, of which upper Tweeddale formed part in the Dark Ages. Many arguments have been put forward for the area around Stobo and Drumelzier having associations with Arthur. Further information on this fascinating subject can be found in works by Professor Veitch, or condensed in an excellent booklet published locally, *Arthur & Merlin: The Tweedale Connection* by John Randall.

This leads us to Merlin whose grave is by tradition to be found where the Poswail Burn joins the Tweed on the haugh below Drumelzier Kirk. But this is not Arthur's bard Merlin Ambrosious; Tweeddale's Merlin is Caledonius, Sylvestris or Merlin the Wild who lived in the century after Arthur. Following Arthur's death, the Celtic race in what is now the Border Country, divided into two factions, one Roman and Christian in outlook, the other to which Merlin belonged, clung to the ancient Celtic beliefs. This latter group was defeated by the former in 573 at Arthuret near Carlisle.

At this battle Merlin's leader, Gwendoleu, had been slain and the grief-stricken bard roamed the hills and valleys of Tweeddale in mourning, living off the land, communing more with the animals of the forest than with his fellow men and when he did do so, only talked of doom and despair for his lost leader and culture. It is suggested by none other than Nikolai Tolstoy that Merlin spent much of his time at a Celtic holy place of spring water and hazel groves at Arthur's Seat on Hart Fell, or Geddes Well on Broad Law, both not distant from Drumelzier.

Meantime following his victory at Arthuret, Rhydderch Hael, leader of the Christian Britons, summoned or recalled St Kentrigen or Mungo from Wales to continue to spread the Gospel in Tweeddale. Tradition has it that Mungo met the wild wandering Merlin at Alterstane in the parish of Stobo and here converted him to the Christian faith. Merlin was to die the following day at Drumelzier, where he was stoned by local shepherds, causing him to stumble into the Tweed where he was impaled on a stake used to anchor fishing nets and subsequently drowned.

A thorn tree has always been associated with the spot where Merlin was buried; a bush still exists where Poswail joins the Tweed, but then these are common in this part of the world. Yet the story does not end here for we return to Thomas the Rhymer of Ecrildoune who was encountered in *Discovering the Borders 1*. Among other predictions made by this shadowy figure were:

> When Tweed and Pausayl meet at Merlin's Grave,
> Scotland shall one monarch have.

This prediction is said to have been fulfilled on the day that James VI was crowned king of England when a flood swept through the Tweed valley and brought the two streams together at the precise spot.

The castles of Drumelzier and Tinnis once formed a vital link in the chain of fortresses which reached downstream through the Tweed valley right to Berwick. Now barely heaps of rubble, there is little to indicate that the Tweedies of Drumelzier and Tinnis once ruled here with absolute authority. Among others, two of the Tweedie clan were said to have taken part in the murder of Rizzio in Holyrood Palace at Edinburgh and seem to have been at odds with their neighbours at home and in the capital. A James Tweedie of Drumelzier was shot during an Edinburgh street brawl, while in 1612 the years of mutual dislike between the Tweedie family and the Vietches of Dawyck flared up when the two lairds met beside the Tweed. Single combat ensued, ending when the Tweedie blood stained the hawthorn blossom where the laird of Drumelzier had fallen to Vietch's sword.

Eventually the land will reclaim the once proud piles of Drumelzier and Tinnis as has been the fate of the weaving hamlet of Linkumdoddie, alleged to have occupied a site on the haugh beside the Tweed opposite Kingledoors, made famous by Burns in his poem 'Willie Wastle'. What kind of weaver Willie was other than indicated in the poet's reference, that he was a 'wabster gude' we do not know; certainly Burns was not tempted to have a fling with Mrs Wastle.

> He had a wife was dour and din,
> O, tinkler Maidgie was her mither —
> Sic a wife as Willie had,
> I wadna gie a button for her!

Set back a little from the Tweed, astride what is the most uninteresting of all her tributaries, the canal-like Biggar Water, lies the village of Broughton. Here in the village the old kirk has been adapted as 'The John Buchan Centre', part of the Biggar Museum Trust. There can be few indeed who have not heard of John Buchan; his novel *The Thirty Nine Steps* was a forerunner of many modern spy thriller, mystery works of fiction. Buchan never lived at Broughton or indeed in the Tweed valley on a permanent basis but such was his love for this upland country that upon his elevation to the peerage he chose for his title Lord Tweedsmuir.

Buchan's grandfather had arrived in 1835 at Peebles to act as temporary assistant to the Town Clerk and stayed a lifetime. His son, also John Buchan, had started studying law but instead felt the call to the ministry, and after study at St Andrews, he was eventually licensed to preach in 1873. One of his first pastoral callings was to Broughton where the incumbent of that parish was abroad for health reasons. Among the congregation was Helen Masterton, daughter of a farmer in Broughton who John Buchan courted and married. Their son, the future Lord Tweedsmuir, was born on 26th August, 1875.

By this time the Rev. John Buchan had been called to Knox Church in Perth where, and later at Glasgow, he spent his working life, only returning to Peebles on a permanent basis on his retirement. Of course the family must have visited many times on holiday and, especially for our John Buchan, this was paradise on earth. Fishing in the hill burns, like on his hill-walking escapades, he ventured further and further afield as he grew up. Long days with the shepherds and country folk ensured that Buchan would not only be a master of the written word in English but excelled also at the Border dialect. Not that all his fishing outings were legal; there were times when Buchan joined clandestine outings with torch and liester to spear salmon on the gravel redds. His poem 'Fisher Jamie' was written in memory of a fallen comrade in 1916.

> Puir Jamie's killed. A better lad
> Ye wadna find tae busk a flee
> Or burn a pule or wield a gad
> Frae Berwick tae the Clints o' Dee.

> I picter him at gloamin' tide
> Steekin' the backdoor o' his hame
> And hastin to the waterside
> To play again the auld auld game;

> And syne wi' saumon on his back,
> Catch't clean against the Heavenly law,
> And Heavenly byliffs on his track
> Gaun linkin' doun some Heavenly shaw.

Perhaps Fisher Jamie was one of Buchan's companions when he was caught in the act of poaching and when only his youth or the fact that his Uncle Will was the procurator fiscal in Peebles saved him from being brought to trial.

Perhaps the popularity of the much filmed *The Thirty Nine Steps* has overshadowed John Buchan's other fictional works. His *John MacNab*, of course, has also remained a classic — the act of taking a salmon, stag and grouse in one day yet goes under the title of a MacNab. In *Witch Wood*, Broughton becomes the village of Woodilee where the young minister David Sempill is set with the task of tackling the pagan rites which are still celebrated in the Black Wood. His task is made no easier by the wall of silence and secrecy maintained by the villagers but he is helped by a beautiful maiden and Montrose gallops briefly through the pages.

Scenes in Buchan's novels cover much of the Border country. *Burnet of Barns* is of course the Barns beside the Manor Water, where the hero stravaigs the Tweeddale hills and beyond to the Low Countries in his adventures. *The Free Fishers* takes the road from Fife through the Cheviots to Norfolk in a Napoleonic spy story. Other tales are set abroad — Africa, where he travelled extensively, and Canada, where of course he was appointed Governor-General.

There is no doubt that John Buchan led an extremely busy life; over and above his writing, a leaflet from the John Buchan Centre describes him as 'lawyer, politician, soldier, historian and biographer'. On display at The John Buchan Centre are many artifacts and manuscripts tracing the life of Lord Tweedsmuir, who even if he was not Tweeddale born was ever a native at heart.

Perhaps we forgot to mention *Greenmantle* among the John Buchan novels, yet it is remembered nearby in Greenmantle Ale produced by The Broughton Brewery Limited. In the latter parts of the 1970s beer drinkers were beginning to rebel against the products of the major breweries who had ceased to brew, or were contemplating stopping brewing, traditional cask-conditioned ales. Campaigns by the Real Ale Society slowed down this trend but it became an opportunity for the establishment of small breweries producing the ale the drinker wanted rather than dictating what should be consumed. Broughton Brewery was the first and is the largest of these new independent breweries.

It may be the first and newest but the name behind it comes from one of the oldest brewing families in Scotland, Younger — in this instance David Younger, whose grandfather's great-grandfather, George Younger, sent regular consignments of his Old Edinburgh Ale to London where the dark brown brew was, it seems, deeply appreciated. Old Jock Scotch Ale is considered the nearest recipe to the Old Edinburgh Ale of yesteryear and Greenmantle remains the flagship with the range completed by Merlin's Ale and Scottish Oatmeal Stout.

Returning to Tweedside, Tweedsmuir is the most upstream of the villages in the upper part of Tweeddale. Like Stobo and Drumelzier it is today but a few houses, a farmstead and kirk. On the way the old coaching establishment of the Crook Inn can supply satisfaction for hunger and thirst and tourist information is also dispensed from a building said to have been there since the time when James VI sallied south to claim the crown of England.

At Tweedsmuir the first kirk was built around the time of the Solemn League and Covenant in 1643, but other earlier religious houses had existed in the now flooded Fruid, while a cell of Crispin the hermit was located at Kingledores nearby. The present building dates from 1874 where in the porch a unique war memorial records the names and photographic likenesses of the Tweedsmuir men who fell in the 1914–18 war, the oak used in the memorial coming from a tree planted by Sir Walter Scott at Abbotsford.

One of the most famous gravestones in the Borders can be seen in the Tweedsmuir kirkyard dedicated to John Hunter:

> J.H. 1660–1685 Here lyes John Hunter martyr who was cruelly murdered at Core head by Col James Douglas and his party for his adherence to the word of God and Scotland's covenanted work of reformation 1685, erected in the year 1726.

A further stone and inscription were placed in 1910 giving a more detailed account of the incident. The inscription on the stone is said to have been relettered by Robert Patterson upon whom Scott based his character 'Old Mortality'.

Near the gates to the kirk yard another stone is dedicated to the memory of twentieth-century martyrs who died in the cause of progress and profit during the construction of the Talla Reservoir. It is all the more poignant that the stone was paid for by the rough navvies who built the dam and civil engineering works, who although in many instances were far from home and living in primitive conditions, could still spare a thought and a shilling for their fallen comrades:

TO THE MEMORY OF
THE MEN WHO DIED
DURING THE PROGRESS
OF THE
TALLA WATERWORKS
1895–1905
OF WHOM OVER THIRTY
ARE INTERRED
IN THIS CHURCHYARD


ERECTED BY THEIR
FELLOW-WORKMEN
AND OTHERS.

The smallest school in Scotland.

Talla is the oldest of the Edinburgh waterworks, fed by a stream of the same name tumbling over Talla Linns. The noise of the falls is said to have failed to drown the arguing voices of those attending a three-day conventicle in 1682 when the voices of the Covenanters were raised discussing the finer points of their beliefs. The wild road from Talla Linns continues over into Megget, then St Mary's Loch. Megget, the most recent of the Border reservoirs, happily was built without the loss of a single workman's life.

Beyond Tweedsmuir the character of what is now the infant Tweed is now changing; moorland presses in alongside the river banks, much of it now replaced with softwood plantations. Beside the road at Tweedhopefoot stands what was once the smallest school in Scotland — little more than a tiny hut with desks for six pupils — which once instilled the three Rs into the children of the outlying farms and holdings here in the upper valley of the Tweed.

Now we are nearing the source of the river whose course has witnessed so much of the history of Scotland and England; a sign by the road marks the source of the River Tweed. On the map the spot is described as 'Tweed Wells', where several trickles of water rising from a boggy bottom combining to form a distinct pool. Ditch-like, the waters trickle eastwards gathering tributaries, first small, then greater, to form the fairest river in the land. Westwards the land rises to the watershed with Annandale, at the Devil's Beeftub, ends our journey in *Discovering the Borders 2*.

# Further Reading List

*The Verge of Scotland*: W.T. Palmer: Robert Hale, London

*Tales of a Grandfather*: Scott

*The Poetical Works of Sir Walter Scott*: Scott

*The Scott Country*: Crockett: A & C Black, London

*Companion to the Tweed*: G Burnett: Methuen and Co., London

*The Steel Bonnets*: G.M. Fraser: Barrie & Jenkins, London

*One Woman and her Dog*: Viv Billingham

*The Proceedings of the Berkwickshire Naturalists' Club*

*District Guides to Roxburgh, Ettrick and Lauderdale and Tweedale*

*Companion to Hawick and District*: R.E. Scott, Hawick Community
Council

*Flower of the Forest: Selkirk a new History*: John M. Gilbert: Selkirk
Common Good Fund

*Pamphlets and guides to local festivals* e.g., *Braw Lads Gathering* and
*Beltane*

*The Ballads of Scotland*, Vol. 1. Aytoun

*Discovering the Borders*, 1. Spence. John Donald

177

# Index